The
Presumption
of Culture

The Presumption of Culture

Structure, Strategy, and Survival
in the Canadian Cultural Landscape

Tom Henighan

RAINCOAST BOOKS
Vancouver

To the old gang at *Ottawa Revue*

Copyright © 1996 by Tom Henighan

First published in 1996 by
Raincoast Book Distribution Ltd.
8680 Cambie Street
Vancouver, B.C.
V6P 6M9
(604) 323-7100

10 9 8 7 6 5 4 3 2 1

CANADIAN CATALOGUING IN PUBLICATION DATA

Henighan, Tom.
The presumption of culture

Includes bibliographical references and index.
ISBN 1-55192-013-1

1. Arts, Canadian. 2. Canada – Civilization – 1945- 3.
Canada – Intellectual life. 4. Canada – Cultural policy. I.
Title.

NX513.A1H46 1996 700'.971'09049 C95-911097-6

Designed by Dean Allen
Project Editor: Michael Carroll
Copy Editor: Dallas Harrison

Printed and bound in Canada

Contents

Acknowledgements

I HAD NO GRANT, research assistant, or sabbatical in which to work on this book, but at the very beginning, Jason Green found and helped me to organize some of the many newspaper clippings I consulted. I want to thank Carol Barton of the Canada Council library, and reference librarians of the Ottawa Public Library, for steering me to books and reports. I am indebted to my friends Pat and Bill Milliken, and to Rick Taylor, for their usual warm support. And I am also indebted to my sons, Stephen and Michael Henighan; to my daughter, Phoebe; and to my wife, Marilyn Carson. As for those in the cultural community who contributed, they and I have agreed that my gratitude can best be expressed privately. For work on my text I want to thank Dallas Harrison and Rachelle Kanefsky. Finally I must acknowledge my great debt to Raincoast's managing editor, Michael Carroll, for his interest in this project and for overseeing the whole thing with unerring skill, patience, and positive energy.

Introduction: Crisis in the Arts

Without contraries, there is no progression.
  – William Blake, *The Marriage of Heaven and Hell*

AS WE MOVE toward the 21st century, Canada has a thriving culture. Our writers, musicians, artists, and filmmakers have established themselves as a powerful creative force in the international cultural community to an extent that would have seemed impossible 45
years ago. Yet Canadian culture, in the mid-nineties, appears to be in crisis: scarcely a week goes by without bad news in the arts community,
usually involving budget cuts, cancellation of new projects, and closures
– though more subtle threats, involving demographic and technological
changes, appear from time to time.

Anyone who looks closely at the Canadian situation can find plausible reasons for the instability of what appears to be a flourishing artistic life in our country. First, Canadian artistic growth was, by and large,
seeded by government funding, both federal and provincial. Over the
past decade, this funding has been eroded, in line with budgetary cutbacks of other programs. This in itself might not have been a problem,
but *no real attempt has been made to adjust the structures set up to administer
that funding.* We have no federal ministry of culture; the various arts and
culture portfolios have been passed from the Secretary of State to the
Department of Communications to Canadian Heritage, almost as if no
one has known what to do with them. There are still major tensions
between federal and provincial governments (and between national and
regional agendas) in the sphere of arts funding and control, and the
issue of Quebec culture (special or separate?) has not been resolved.
The Canada Council is clearly in decline, yet no creative changes in
structure have been proposed. The CBC seems to go from one absurd

instability to the next; such instability would have been avoided if any of the recent governments in power had created a strong corporate policy within an overall cultural plan.

Second, *the arts community itself has changed its focus*. The nationalistic fervour that carried us through the sixties and seventies has given way to factionalism and the most divisive kind of political activism. More and more we see artists identifying with political causes and ideologies, using art as a means of political expression rather than creating works that express more central human values.

Third, though educational levels in Canada have improved enormously over the past few decades, *there has been no dramatic change in either the number or the quality of Canadian audiences for the arts*; in fact, many people believe that the public in Canada is more indifferent to the arts than ever before, more ignorant of what role the arts and culture might (and must) play in their lives.

The purpose of this book is simply to address some of these issues directly and to offer a few solutions. In the course of doing so, I will take a stand on some central issues, but it will be as well to make my position clear before I start.

First, what do I mean by "culture"? The word, of course, is ambiguous. The Task Force on Professional Training for the Cultural Sector in Canada suggested four distinct meanings for the word *culture,* including, first, one's personal knowledge, beliefs, values, et cetera; second, the anthropological sense of a cultural community; third, "cultivated culture," i.e., what a person knows of his or her cultural tradition; and fourth, culture as art.[1] It is the latter two notions that are the subject of this book.

Yet there is another definition at stake. Does "culture" include only the traditional fine arts, or does it include everything, including pop music, comic books, Harlequin romances, et cetera? The common and (to me) irritating way of distinguishing between the fine arts and the more popular, generally accessible, kind is to adopt the terms "high" (i.e., serious artistic) culture and "low" (i.e., mass) culture. Or, just as bad, "elite" culture and "popular" culture. To get away from this labelling, I often use the term "aesthetic culture" to refer to "high" culture, and "entertainment culture" to refer to "low" culture. I use the term "aesthetic culture" to refer to Bach, Shakespeare, James Joyce, Balanchine, Margaret Atwood, the Group of Seven, and so on, not because their works are not entertaining but because they are relatively complex, and part of specific historical or aesthetic traditions. Such works often require from us some education (it can be self-education), experience, or development of taste before a good level of communication ensues. I use the term "entertainment culture" to refer to works that we assume (not always correctly) have more immediate appeal and "direct entertainment value," for example, the Beatles, *Star Wars,* Bryan Adams, et cetera. I don't always prefer aesthetic culture to entertainment culture. I would not be alone among classical music listeners in preferring an evening of Duke Ellington to an evening of Ernst Toch, nor among "serious" readers in preferring Dashiell Hammett to the latest self-indulgent avant-garde novel. The products of human creativity don't invite the correlation "serious" equals "always profound and worthy," or "entertainment" equals "always superficial and inferior." (As Kurt Weill, the composer, put it, "good light music is . . . more valuable than bad serious music.") Between "serious" and "popular" there is, in fact, a continuum of values, techniques, objectives, and audiences (while the art of today, in our "postmodern" era, often mixes high and low in sometimes inventive, sometimes disconcerting ways).

Yet pure aesthetic culture means a great deal to me and is something I think worth explaining and defending. I see no reason to apologize for it. As for the terms I have chosen, well, no terms can be foolproof or perfect, but I feel comfortable with mine.

The second issue is: how do I regard culture? I regard culture as one of the essentials of any good society; in most respects it is as important as health, education, and welfare in making life worth living for all citizens. It is my presumption, in other words, that culture is a social necessity and that aesthetic culture in particular has the power to speak to everyone. Unfortunately – and I think quite wrongly – some people consider such a view presumptuous. Some people are unaware of the value of culture. Yet culture works for people whether they know it or not. I believe, therefore, that the state should support culture in various ways, including dispensing the taxpayer's money to keep it alive.

I disagree completely with the conservative or laissez-faire position that the state has no business funding culture. I do not believe that cultural matters should be left to the "free market" (if one exists), or to the majority vote; culture is far too important for that.[2] One of the main themes of this book is that if Canada stops supporting its culture, it will be endangering its survival as an independent nation. Some argue (to me, incredibly) that there is no such thing as an identifiable, distinct Canadian culture.[3] I wonder, then, what they think has been going on in this country over the past several decades, and even before? What about *The Jack Pine* or *The Edge of the Maple Wood*; what about *Surfacing* and *The Diviners*; what about Glenn Gould and Leonard Cohen, or

Gordon Lightfoot, Peter Gzowski, Farley Mowat, Douglas Cardinal, and Robert Lepage?

Cultural nationalism, in some quarters, seems to have a bad name. I can understand this, if by cultural nationalism is meant the support of culture in order to glorify or prop up the state.[4] My own view is that distinct national identities do come about, that they spring from the activities of many creative people working in individual ways, according to the demands of their own creative impulses. Yet because these people connect in space and time, and often in language, because they are influenced by subtle common factors of environment and tradition, it is quite possible to speak of national traditions, national energies, national visions.

My belief is that the Canadian national vision, made manifest, articulated, and shaped by its culture, is in danger, and that the danger is coming from the "universal entertainment culture" that is largely a product of American industry. (America is in danger from this, too – the older, more cultivated America.) Because our own entertainment culture has been largely (though not totally) co-opted by this American-style popcult, I believe that Canadian aesthetic culture (and to some extent our more distinctively Canadian popular culture) represent the best national defence Canada has against assimilation into the American cultural hegemony.

Those who argue in favour of a laissez-faire position of government in regard to culture seem to me to be risking the destruction of Canadian culture and therefore of Canada as we know it. Equally those who insist on the Marxist defamation of aesthetic culture as "elitist," those who are determined to overthrow quality in the name of equality, seem to me to risk the future of Canada, because they are in the process of undermining our distinctive national culture in favour of a factional culture based on interest groups and ideological positions rather than acknowledging those historical continuities that (despite the "sins" of history) hold us together.[5]

Many academics who speak and write of art, and artists who espouse ideological positions, have made us suspicious of the old notions of greatness in art; they have attacked the Western tradition of excellence, and cast doubt even on the language with which we have sought to express the powerful and cleansing idealism implicit in the artistic experience at its finest and purest. Their palaver is reminiscent of the sour voices that once told us that good novels had to be unreadable and good music cacophonous. A new circle in Dante's hell should be invented for all such scoffers: the circle of the debasers of the truth of art.

What is that truth? It is that great art speaks to the heart of the human condition, and though it can be understood as part of history and as the expression of a certain individual in a certain place, it transcends its origins and touches the universal – otherwise it remains a mere document, a historical artifact of limited usefulness and interest. There is a canon of great artworks that rises above the interests of any class or group, and if we fail to sustain contact with that canon, we destroy our culture.[6]

This is not a truth we hear much of in the academies these days, and the reasons are evident. Because the official right and left seem to have spent the last half century systematically discrediting themselves, political radicalism has been relocated in universities and artistic circles, where it remains purely theoretical – and therefore impotent. Theoreticians and creators made cynical by philosophical doctrines of mechanism and reductionism, and fed by the pseudo-religion of Marxism, have delighted in "exposing" every treasured assumption of the hated past. These politically frustrated inactivists and their ideological allies have moved away from both the concrete and the aspirational sides of art and have landed us in a dreary wasteland of their own imagining, where nothing exists except human power (exercised always as oppression). In this kingdom every ideal is tainted, and the evil father rules, thrice murdered (by Darwin, Marx, and Freud), yet still fettering his powerless children.

I am not suggesting, of course, that the purpose of the arts is merely to uplift us, or that art should not deal with human evil – quite the contrary. Nor am I suggesting that a nation should not support access to the arts for all its people. It is simply time, I believe, to get back to a balanced view of our traditions, to stop sneering at the greatness of our European inheritance in favour of every kind of alternative. It is time to train our children to know and love the classic, canonical works that have made our civilization the envy of the world. The purpose of this book is to suggest ways in which our culture can be preserved and enhanced through a balance of government reforms of existing arts and educational structures, through contributions from the private sector, and through the efforts of artists themselves.

It is clear that the seed time is over for contemporary Canadian culture. It is time now for the maturing of ideas, of organizational forms, of thrusts in education – all carried out with the notion that there will not be much new funding for these activities. There must be changes, and they must be much more than ad hoc solutions. What is at stake is the survival of our culture, and quite possibly of Canada itself.

EVEN AS I COMPLETE WORK on the proofs of this book, the state of the arts and culture in Canada continues to be major news. Michel Dupuy has been replaced as minister of Canadian Heritage by the more outspoken

Sheila Copps, who – judging by her initial statements – seems to have been encouraged by the prime minister to invoke and develop cultural issues as a means of strengthening national unity. After the close call of the Quebec referendum, and perhaps because of the complaints of many federalists about the lack of passion and visionary power in the government's presentation of its case for a unified Canada, during the coming months we can expect to see much made of the power of the arts to enrich our sense of nationhood.

Meanwhile, the long-awaited Juneau Report has appeared, and while it is too early to judge in-depth, it appears to be a bold attempt to reinvent CBC Television and to put it on a firm basis for the future. Among its 95 recommendations the report suggests protection for CBC Radio, fewer television sports broadcasts, more TV arts and education, more regional input, and withdrawal from competition for TV advertising – all of which would go far toward creating the kind of national public broadcasting that I advocate in these pages. The report, in fact, offers Sheila Copps and CBC president Perrin Beatty a chance to challenge the Canadian public to accept specific levies on telecommunications services in the name of securing a strong CBC, an option that has already met with considerable hostility from all quarters.

The Juneau Report is also very constructive on Telefilm Canada and, if implementation occurs, we may see an even richer development of Canadian feature films; while the National Film Board has been told to centre more effort on production and less on distribution and marketing.

Another major issue that has surfaced in recent months concerns private-sector financing of the arts. Should arts organizations accept sponsorship from tobacco companies, even though such sponsorship may be banned by the federal government, and in view of the moral distaste in which many hold this industry? Also, should the federal and provincial governments accept funding from American private interests that wish to buy their way into the Canadian market, funding that would offer, in some cases, millions of dollars for the arts and culture yet, in fact, would be in the nature of a bribe to gain exemption from Canadian regulations? The U.S.-controlled Viacom and BC TELECOM corporations have raised precisely this issue – offering huge grants in exchange for such "considerations" – and it is one to ponder as we explore new avenues of private-sector support for the arts.

Such issues confirm what I point out in the pages that follow, that there is a pressing need in Canada in the nineties for a total revisioning of arts policy, one that will include a set of national goals and result in federal restructuring and in legislation that will secure the ideals of our country and our culture into the next century.

1 The Introverted Culture and the Great Awakening

God help the Minister who meddles in art!
  – Lord Melbourne, speech to the British Parliament

C ANADA IN THE FIRST HALF of the 20th century: the stable, the comfortable, the quiet, the unassuming, the *invisible* North. Generations of English Canadians learned to live with such an image of their country; travelling abroad, constantly mistaken for Americans, some attempted to define themselves, but most simply shrugged their shoulders and smiled, content to wear the mask of pleasant anonymity, to be pseudo-Yankees. If Canada meant anything to non-Canadians, it meant harsh winters: "How can you stand it? I couldn't live there myself!" This refrain was heard often, in London, New York, and Paris. Quebec was a curious fact that intrigued many non-Canadians, but only up to a point, and the Canadian traveller, whether francophone or anglophone, was unlikely to dive into that complex issue. Of course, there was hockey, the Dionne quintuplets, Barbara Anne Scott, and Anne of Green Gables. But after that, not much. And so it went, right through the thirties, forties, and fifties.

What odd times those were for Canada, those decades of provinciality and nonexistence. What a strange country our parents and grandparents inhabited! John Gray, the Canadian playwright who grew up in Truro, Nova Scotia, in the late fifties, once testified to the repressed, and oppressed, nature of the Canadian cultural psyche in the years before the Great Awakening. For Gray and his young friends,

> the world was a distant flame from the south. The flame glowed brightly when we went to the movies, or watched television, or listened to the hit parade; but as soon as the movie was over, we were back in Truro, which seemed more cold and drab than it had ever been. I mean, what was the Truro Music Festival compared to Elvis Presley?[1]

Gray gives a powerful picture of growing up on a steady diet of American and British history, of studying English literature that bore little relation to his everyday experience. He took it for granted that Canada had little art and culture, and that what little it did have was lifeless, dull, and insignificant.

> If there was one overwhelming lesson to be learned from both my
> school lessons and from my out-of-school experiences . . . it was the
> notion that culture, history and the arts are things that come from some-
> place else. . . . Canada is the one place in the world where nothing hap-
> pens. A cold, drab lifeless place, grateful for any warmth and light it can
> get from that distant flame.[2]

Going on to university did not change things for Gray. "When I received my degree in 1968," he tells us,

> I had still managed never to have consciously read a Canadian book. I
> had never seen or read a Canadian play, and although I had been playing
> with rock bands for five years, I had never, to my knowledge, heard or
> played a Canadian song. Could a graduate of any other university in the
> world make such a claim about the history and culture of his or her own
> country? And yet it never occurred to me that it mattered.[3]

Gray's experience was hardly unique. After the Second World War, it was becoming clear to a few knowledgeable Canadians that as far as culture was concerned, Canada could almost be considered a desert. Countries with equally small populations and facing somewhat similar cultural pressures – the Scandinavian countries notably – had made by then a relatively large impact on the international cultural scene. Ibsen, Sibelius, Grieg, and Hamsun were known to almost everyone; Ingmar Bergman was in ascent on the world cultural horizon. In Canada there was the Canadian Broadcasting Corporation (CBC), created in 1936, and the National Film Board (NFB), founded in 1939, but it was no surprise to informed Canadians when the Massey-Lévesque Commission in 1951 suggested that our cultural landscape had to be characterized as virtually in a state of arrested development.

The Massey Commission itself (the Royal Commission on National Development in the Arts, Letters, and Sciences) was a peculiarly Canadian phenomenon: an elite group instructed by Louis St. Laurent's government to survey the cultural scene and to make recommendations for improvement.[4] The commission's report – eloquent, incisive, and strongly suggestive of creative change – makes good reading even today. Yet the picture painted will likely leave one incredulous. Were things really that bad? Could there have been only *14* works of fiction published in English Canada in 1951? Were there really only three or four professional theatre companies? *In the whole country?* Were musical performances mainly carried out in church basements and school gymnasiums? The answer, amazingly, is "Yes."

Of course, no one could suggest that a country that had already produced painters like J.W. Morrice, the Group of Seven, and Tom Thomson, film directors like Allan Dwan and a host of Hollywood talent, poets like Emile Nelligan, St. Denys Garneau, and Archibald Lampman, a writer like Stephen Leacock, a musician like Ernest MacMillan – no one could suggest that such a country was an artistically barren wasteland. There is a difference, however, between the springing up of representative artists and the flowering of a whole culture, a difference between a country whose fame rests on individual – and often amateur – talent, and a country that has created artistic work, as well as institutions and traditions, that the world begins to recognize as unique and enduring.

Today, when Canada has novelists in virtually every town and hamlet, not to mention the population explosion of published fiction writers in our major cities, we can afford a certain complacency – even though, as we shall see, our present cultural problems are monumental. Nonetheless there is no more talk of a "desert." We have, indeed, a substantial culture: at least 30 professional orchestras that play classical music, over 160 publishing houses, 30 or so dance companies, 65 organizations producing and distributing films and videos, more than 50 artists' centres, over 80 public art galleries, and approximately 100 cultural periodicals. In addition Canada in the nineties displays a cultural mosaic that includes artists from roots unrecognized or nonexistent in the fifties.

The Massey-Lévesque Commission report, when analyzing the barrenness of Canadian culture, pointed significantly to the "vast importations" of foreign artistic material, thus confirming the experience of Canadians such as John Gray, who would later look back upon a childhood of colonized near helplessness. The report quoted with approval a submission from the Canadian Writers' Committee: "A mass of outside values is dumped into our cities and towns and homes.... We would like to see the development of a little Canadian independence, some say in who we are, and what we think and how we feel and what we do.... The fault is not America's, but ours."[5] A very modest and, one might say, very Canadian clarion call! Nonetheless, the commission recommended wisely. As a result of its recommendations, the National Library of Canada was created (1953) to conserve the past, and the Canada Council (1957) to seed the future.

For several good reasons, the Massey-Lévesque Commission can be cited as a central milestone in Canada's cultural history. As the first major government act of intervention in cultural development after the Second World War, it carried on and solidified the tradition of "guided development," implicitly suggesting that the free play of market forces could not be allowed to carry the day in the areas of art, science, and communication. Such a policy derived logically not only from the 19th-century federal and provincial endowments of museums and galleries but also from the federal attention to broadcasting and film in the thirties. The Massey-Lévesque Commission paved the way for a whole series of royal commissions – on broadcasting (1957), on publications (i.e., magazines, 1961), on the mass media (1970), on book publishing (1972), all of which culminated in the Federal Cultural Policy Review Committee of 1982 (the influential Applebaum-Hébert report).

In a larger context, what we can now see emerging out of the Massey-Lévesque Commission deliberations is the notion that culture and arts are not simply aesthetic delights, not simply noble ideals that can be life enhancing for those who experience them, but also a national necessity, that a nation without a strong indigenous culture is threatened with extinction. "We are defending civilization," the report argues, "our share of it, our contribution to it. The things with which our inquiry deals are the elements which give civilization its character and its meaning. It would be paradoxical to defend something which we are unwilling to strengthen and enrich, and which we would even allow to decline."[6]

A great deal of past culture, at least in Western society, came about thanks to private patronage. Well into the 20th century, princes and courts, rich merchants and bourgeois millionaires, paid for some of the great art of the West.[7] A monied elite created artifacts and entertainments for its own pleasure – and this elitism still hangs over some aspects of our culture, largely to its detriment. Also, beginning with the Romantics in the early 19th century, a sense of art as leading away from the crude realities of nature and society appeared. Somewhat later, the art-for-art's-sake movement set the creator (poet, painter, or musician) against the materialism and mechanism that some thinkers (and most of the middle class) saw as "progress." Both trends, private financing and the aesthetic movement, suggested that art was something distinct from – and far above – ordinary life, out of reach of the ordinary citizen. Art and culture, in such circumstances, threatened to remain the recreations of an elite, the arcane pleasures of a gifted minority, having little to do with social development in the broad sense.

Yet set against this notion of the exclusiveness of art there arose the sense of art and culture as morally central to common social life, as the carriers of values and visions that could serve the whole society. The seeming decline of organized religion suggested that art was the last refuge of "spiritual" values, too important to be left to a minority of the wealthy, too powerful an instrument of vision to be reserved for the visionaries. Thinkers in a tradition stretching from Matthew Arnold through Lewis Mumford and, in a narrower vein, Allan Bloom and Neil Postman have argued that a modern society without art, without culture, would be ill defined, barren, and without goals, literally pointless if not actually inhumane, because it would be doomed to ignore or forget real values and misunderstand the true interrelationships of the person, the group, the ideal.

The Massey-Lévesque commissioners looked around them and saw in Canada not only a nation with its own character and history, but one that was threatened by a massive influx of foreign values, images, and ideas – especially from the giant to the south. In time these ideas, images, and values would certainly obliterate the developing Canadian consciousness, our fragile national self-awareness. With its small population and its lack of massive sources of private funding, Canada was at risk, but culture could actually be the instrument of our defence – if the federal government intervened to promote it. The Massey-Lévesque Commission, with many dutiful nods to the old elitism, the old laissez-faire, opted for culture and arts as instruments of social animation and national survival. Only through a development of its cultural industries could Canada hope to resist the Americanization that threatened it. Any idea of a completely free market could only mean national suicide. Thus, the Canada Council was created to support the arts and social sciences (it originally did minister to both), and the government assumed a considerable share of the cost of supporting culture in this country.

Indeed, the famous Canadian penchant for compromise shows up in the mode of arts funding that has become commonplace in Canada since the Second World War, a policy borrowed from Britain. The assumption of successive governments has been that while it would be unrealistic to rely exclusively on the American model of private support, we cannot go to the other extreme and adopt the common European model of almost total government intervention. For despite an ancient tradition of patronage and exclusiveness in the arts, over the past 200 years most European governments have assumed a larger and larger share of arts funding. The change happened with the rise of republican and bureaucratic elites. Napoleon is reputed to have said: "Complaints are made that we have no literature; this is the fault of the Minister of the Interior." In the United States, on the other hand, private patronage has long been supreme (the National Endowment for the Arts was founded as late as

1965, and has never been regarded as a central source).

When the Canada Council was created in 1957, it was set up as a central, independent agency, at arm's length from government, and its main mission was to support artists and arts organizations. And other ministries and agencies (federal, provincial, local) have, over the years, assumed part of the burden of ensuring the Canadian cultural identity by paying for it and by making policy decisions that develop it. Post-Massey, the mainstay of arts funding in Canada has been government at all levels, and though plenty of room has been left for private initiative, almost nothing has been done to stimulate it (see chapter 8).

Perhaps the most amazing thing about the Massey-Lévesque Commission report is that its recommendations, resulting in government actions and policies of many kinds, appear to have done the job. During the sixties, seventies, and eighties, Canadian culture came to life. There were many reasons for this flowering – economic prosperity, increasing urbanization, and population diversity among them – but the establishment of the Canada Council, the commitment of government funding to the arts, was probably the single most important factor in effecting this change and in sustaining it. The growth of Canadian arts and culture during this period was amazing; even more amazing, perhaps, was the Canadian public's acceptance of this growth. Most Canadians took to heart the Massey formulation that strong arts and culture equal a strong nation. They came forward by the thousands, as if out of nowhere, to recognize and celebrate their artists. Canadian self-identity, our national and regional pride, have since become closely associated with this artistic growth.

The sense of many Canadians growing up in the fifties that they suffered from a disjointed or missing consciousness led them to welcome, with a strong nationalistic rhetoric, the art that began to appear in the sympathetic climate created by the government. Canadians seemed liberated by the change, grateful, no doubt, that the reality they lived in and experienced every day was finally being represented in art and culture, glad to shake off the sense that their inner world was created, fed, and dominated from elsewhere.

The coming-of-age of Canadian culture was marked by many milestones, as well as by a few curious offshoots. I can only point to a handful here, almost randomly chosen. Externally the American involvement in Vietnam helped distance many Canadians from the goals of American foreign policy; it jolted them into the realization that Canada was different. The celebration of Canada's first 100 years of nationhood at Expo 67 in Montreal, with its striking architecture and exhibits, became the focus of a new wave of national pride. Meanwhile the Quiet Revolution had begun in Quebec and was fostering a massive development of francophone culture. Northrop Frye reframed Canadian literature in terms of "the bush garden" (1971), a defensive conception, yet a step beyond the idea of the wasteland uncovered by Massey, while Margaret Atwood's *Survival* (1972) defined the national character in terms of literary strategies and themes: Canadians were taught how not to be victims, either of raw nature or of American imperialism. Atwood began her literary career under the wing of House of Anansi Press in Toronto, only one of a host of small publishing companies born at that time, largely funded by the Canada Council; these companies espoused the new Canadian literature, and nurtured an enthusiastic (and thoroughly nationalistic) conception of the avant-garde.

The late sixties and early seventies saw the emergence in anglophone Montreal of the bardic Leonard Cohen, who bridged serious and popular culture in a peculiarly Canadian way, while Nathan Cohen, the acerbic Toronto theatre critic, set the tone for the creation of a mature Canadian theatre, full of irony and dissonance. On a radio show, Cohen made a cutting remark to a British panelist about his London residence: "That's not much of an address," Cohen said. "Neither is Toronto," came the acidic reply. A few years later, when Toronto had come into its own culturally, such a colonialist riposte would have been impossible. From the sixties onward, Marshall McLuhan was offering challenging ideas about the media, adding something new and striking to the Massey Commission's concept of redeeming content. When McLuhan himself appeared in the famous Woody Allen film *Annie Hall* in 1977, it seemed, almost perversely, proof that Canada was no longer culturally on the defensive. And I recall in Hamburg, in 1961, hearing an American banker's wife enthusing about the new Canadian keyboard sensation, Glenn Gould – the first time I had heard any Canadian artist mentioned by a foreigner, and clearly identified as Canadian.

At this point it is intriguing to turn back to the experiences of John Gray and to learn how he – perhaps a typical young Canadian intellectual of the period – made the transition from colonized consciousness to a new sense of national identity. "By 1974," Gray tells us,

> I was nearly twenty-eight and still had not seen a professionally-produced Canadian play. And I was just as convinced as ever that there was no point, because Canadian culture was dull. Is it any wonder that I had never written or composed anything? What was there for me, a Canadian, to write about that would be worth reading or seeing?[8]

Gray describes how he was dragged by a friend to a Theatre Passe Muraille production done in a rural setting outside of Toronto, a history play actually about Canada, called *1837: The Farmers' Revolt*. Noticing the enthusiasm of the audience of farmers for this Canadian subject matter, Gray searched for and found the gravestones of the teacher and blacksmith heroes of the play, who had been hanged for treason. Making a personal connection between history and art effected a transformation in Gray. "I suppose there are cultures where they don't assume unfamiliarity and alienness as part of the nature of art itself," he writes. "And it would be difficult . . . [for them] . . . to understand what it is to touch something you read about, or see it in a play, for the first time, in your own country, at the age of twenty-eight. . . . I joined Theatre Passe Muraille as a musician and found, for the first time in my life, I could write songs."[9]

This birth of interest in Canadian arts and culture, the sense that many young people had that they were finally meeting art that spoke to their everyday experience in this country, made for an exhilarating, if conflictual, time. I remember in the early seventies sitting in a hotel room in downtown Toronto at a Canada Council jury meeting while two members, one a cultural nationalist and the other an internationalist, screamed insults at each other over a half-consumed bottle of Scotch. Such passion about art in Canada would have been almost unthinkable a decade before. Canadian government policy and funding, the march of history, prosperity that created a surplus of money for the arts – these enabled Canada in the sixties, seventies, and eighties not only to attain a new level of production and quality in the cultural domain but also to begin to achieve, for the first time in its history, a world-class and thus exportable culture, which has gone far toward putting Canada on the global map.

But the miracle did not stop there. In the next phase, which began in the early eighties and is still in progress, the world began to take notice of Canadian achievements. Canadian writers, filmmakers, and musicians have become part of the international scene, and scarcely a week goes by without a triumph of Canadian art on one of the world stages – in New York, San Francisco, London, Paris, Edinburgh, or Berlin. Canadian films travel the world, and Canadian books are reviewed everywhere; Canadian theatre and music and visual art gain respect in all quarters.

In a recent report on culture and foreign policy, essayist John Ralston Saul makes this point vividly. Drawing on his experience of a 1993-94 trip to Britain and France, he points out that while Canadian foreign policy, domestic events, and even sports achievements were not much in view, Canadian arts and culture were everywhere referred to, and often visible:

On book review days there would be Canadian books reviewed promi-
nently in a number of papers. . . . There was a Canadian film enjoying
attention and success in Paris. . . . While an inventive Anglophone opera
director was being lauded at the Aix Festival . . . an astonishing
Francophone Canadian theatre creator was the star at the Edinburgh
Festival. . . . And everywhere I went people were writing or talking about
a film on Glenn Gould.[10]

More important, Saul continues:

> In this same period I didn't come across any other mention of Canada.
> None of our political figures was quoted. No trade victories or battles
> were discussed [clearly Saul's experience preceded the "turbot war"!].
> None of our business leaders were profiled. When important interna-
> tional crises, in which we were very much involved, were reported, our
> role was not even mentioned.

And Saul concludes tellingly:

> The point of this anecdote is that Canada's profile abroad is, for the most
> part, its culture. That is our image. That is what Canada becomes in peo-
> ple's imaginations around the world. . . . Not being a player in interna-
> tional communications today implies disappearing from this planet. It
> isn't simply a lost cultural and financial opportunity. It is a major prob-
> lem for foreign policy. . . . The question is not whether we can afford to
> spend to export culture. The question is whether we can afford not to.[11]

Surely the Massey-Lévesque commissioners would have been amazed
to read such words. They would also, quite justifiably, have congratulated
themselves on a triumph of foresight. Not only did their promotion of
culture as the soul stuff of national identity succeed beyond all measure
in eliciting the pride of Canadians in their homegrown arts and culture;
the commissioners' elegantly phrased 1951 report also precipitated a
development that would eventually give Canada a real presence in the
global community, in a world increasingly dominated by media, image,
and cultural exports.

At this point, however, a Canadian reader with even a cursory interest in the arts will call to mind statistics, incidents, headlines, editorials –
possibly even experiences – that tell a slightly different story about the
development of the arts in Canada over the past several years. We all
know, for example, that the economic downturn of the late eighties and
early nineties has begun to undermine the funding policies that helped
to bring about the "cultural miracle" that I have outlined above. The
baseline of Canada Council funding, for example, has not been increased

by Parliament since 1986, and, taking inflation into account, this has meant a funding decrease of about 30 percent since 1981. The council has begun to remodel itself (cutting personnel and services such as the Art Bank and the Explorations Program), with consequences that are very uncertain. The CBC has been hit with enormous cutbacks, as well as disruptions of leadership, and faces structural transformations that may change its whole focus and nature. Telefilm Canada, the National Ballet, the Montreal, Toronto, and Vancouver symphonies, in the past four or five years, have all suffered major crises, mostly having to do with under-funding. While Stratford has been turning to musical comedies and Gilbert and Sullivan to help balance its budget, Harbourfront in Toronto (one of Canada's most important multipurpose arts facilities) has been threatened with closure, and the National Arts Centre in Ottawa has never really lived up to the promise of the sixties. In 1992 the Art Gallery of Ontario had to close its doors for several months; the much-needed opera-ballet centre in Toronto, talked about by successive federal and Ontario provincial governments, shows no signs of being built. These are merely the most visible signs of a general crisis affecting theatre compa-nies, small publishing houses, galleries, and artists' groups from the Maritimes to Vancouver Island, symptoms of a malaise that threatens to undermine further progress toward Canadian national development in the arts.

Nor is the crisis simply a matter of funding. Until a short time ago, most Canadians assumed that our particular economic and social mix, our underlying social structures, and our balance of urban and rural com-ponents, of linguistic and regional interests, left little to be desired. In recent years a number of controversies in the cultural sphere have upset such complacency: these include boycotts by First Nations groups of exhibitions regarded as offensive to tribal traditions; protests by racially sensitive groups over the Royal Ontario Museum's exhibition *Into the Heart of Africa*; shouting matches at Writers' Union meetings over ques-tions of writers and race; the introduction of blatantly political and ide-ological criteria into the choice of exhibitions and programs every-where; and the emergence of sinister co-optings of expression disguised by polite terms that nonetheless smack of an Orwellian nightmare, terms such as "appropriation of voice" and "political correctness." If the *appa-ratchiki* of the left have been busy leading the arts into the promised land of correct politics, conservatives have been equally active, lamenting funds wasted on "artists who refuse to get a job," occasionally promoting censorship, and suggesting, against all historical plausibility, that arts and culture in Canada can do very well without any government support.

Although some government surveys offer an optimistic view of the attachment of the Canadian public to the arts, there are sobering counterindications. For example, in 1951 there were about 189,000 Canadians with university degrees; by 1991 there were 2.4 million. While audiences for the arts also increased during the same period, the increases were far below the increase in university education.[12] This discrepancy suggests that, contrary to the assumptions of many casual observers, higher education has done much less than expected to increase arts sensitivity in Canada. Even more strikingly, the Canadian public, despite decades of what should have been sensitizing activity following the Massey-Lévesque report, seems surprisingly ignorant of, and in fact hostile to, certain aspects of contemporary art and culture. (Unfortunately the more blatant instances of know-nothingism, stupidity, and prejudice are often exploited by reporters, especially television news reporters, seemingly eager to poke fun at culture.) For example, in 1989, when the National Gallery of Canada purchased *Voice of Fire,* an abstract painting by the American Barnett Newman, for $1.8 million, protests resulted in a parliamentary inquiry, while a farmer living south of Ottawa expressed his defiance by producing an oversized replica of the Newman and posting it on a fence beside one of his pig pens. Jana Sterbak's so-called *Flesh Dress* (1991) resulted in a signed petition faxed to M. P. John Cole by members of his Newmarket, Ontario, constituency. The letter reads as follows:

> To John Cole, Member of Parliament:
>
> Whereas the National Gallery of Art ought to show art acceptable to us, and whereas the art it displays reflects on all Canadians, we the undersigned wish it to be known that the artwork described as a woman's dress made of raw beef (1) does not constitute art, (2) does not reflect art concepts, views or norms, (3) is an obscene waste of food representing a needless slaughter of beef, and (4) should be removed forthwith. Be it also known that the curator who approved this display and defended its continuation ought to be replaced.[13]

The question therefore arises: how many Canadians are really deeply committed to the arts? What kind of artworks are they interested in, and what kind of performances are they attending? If the public interest in the arts is so strong, then why aren't there more protests when cutbacks occur? If the National Gallery of Canada, the Vancouver Opera, or the Montreal Symphony closed down tomorrow, how many people would protest? Have those who care about the arts and who try to articulate the importance of culture really got their message across? What message should be conveyed? That the arts and culture are a national necessity?

That they can generate prestige for our country and money for our economy? That life would hardly be worth living without them?

The picture I have painted here is of our national culture rapidly developing so as to become, in a period of 45 years, a player on the world stage. During the same period, however, demographics have been rapidly changing the face of Canada, new technologies are affecting all levels of society, including the practice and distribution of the arts, and new forms of art are emerging as part of this media revolution. The first generation of artists and arts organizations, those who created the contemporary image of Canada for the world, are in full maturity. Moving toward the 21st century, Canada finds itself at a turning point in many ways, and certainly insofar as the arts and culture are concerned. If government fails in its support of the arts, if Canada fails to make good on the achievements of the recent past (and on the great promise of the present), such failure could signify a lost opportunity of major dimensions.

Yet if we believe qualified observers such as Robert Fulford and John Ralston Saul, if we take account of events around us, we must see that, despite nearly 50 years of development, culture in Canada is still very much under siege. The dynamism, the creative energy that can make a place for Canada in the new global consciousness, are certainly threatened, and may well be lost. And if Canada loses quality and the power of self-definition, what is the point of arguing that this country must lay claim to a strong share in the coming world network of communications? Are we perhaps condemning ourselves to plod along the information highway in mechanical fashion, once again the invisible country, with "no expression, nothing to express"? Of what use is the creation of marvellous hardware if we have no content to make it live?

2   Arts, Media, and the Irresistible Future

[M]ight not our current translation of our entire lives into the spiritual form of information seem to make of the entire globe, and of the human family, a single consciousness?
– Marshall McLuhan, *Understanding Media*

THE CANADIAN OF THE YEAR 2010 will experience a world of communications such as past generations could barely imagine. In the 14 years between now and then, a media revolution will take place that will affect all aspects of life for huge numbers of people in North America.

By 2010 entertainment resources, as well as other services, may well be funnelled to the consumer through large-screen, high-definition telecomputers that will dominate a wall of the average middle-class living room. The home screen will serve as a communications centre, combining data, sound, and video. It will be a two-way system, allowing the consumer – for a price – to import information, services, and entertainment, almost without limit. This screen will also be the connecting point to whatever special-interest networks the consumer wishes to access. Video telephone, information retrieval, personalized news reports, shopping, banking and investing, education, library services, routine medical diagnosis, some legal advice, gallery and museum access, concerts and shows of all kinds, not to mention the composition and exchange of original literary, musical, and artistic pieces – these are only a few of the activities that may well be accessed (or in some cases originated) at such terminals. What's more, such activities will feature sound, visual, and print capabilities that will make our present systems look primitive indeed.[1]

This home entertainment and information system (which may contain features not even dreamt of at this writing) will constitute a convergence of the traditional media (broadcast TV, film, radio, and print), a convergence that promises (or threatens) "to create a kind of organic interdependence among the institutions of society," as McLuhan suggested.[2] Will this interdependence mean central control of all information and entertainment by huge corporate interests whose dominance extends far beyond the present reach of even the largest media groups? By the year 2000, the American worldwide "infotainment" industry may account for one dollar out of every six of the global GNP.[3] Can citizens, even governments, hope to exercise any influence in the face of such financial power? One thing is certain: there is no prospect of a "breathing space" between media developments, such as occurred between the introduction of radio and of TV. There will be an almost dizzying rate of change, the speed and complexity of which will defy the abilities of governments to legislate controls and safeguards.

However, we have not yet entered the age of the central information-entertainment pipeline. For the time being, traditional media retain independent lines of contact with the consumer – a situation that should endure through the next decade or so. These traditional media, even apart from future technologies, have great prospects of expansion into the international markets that have come to the fore in the past few years. Expansion around the world, for the time being, runs parallel with technological convergence. Nonetheless, media interrelationships are changing fast (this is clearly visible in the area of television), but even print – seemingly a conservative area – shows evidence of moving toward the predicted convergence. And it is important to note that with each technological advance, there is a shift of the contents. One example: in 1992 the first multimedia books appeared on the market, and the publishing industry is already starting to relate content to the new computer technology. It is possible now, for example, to tailor textbooks to individual university courses; to produce racy novels with the sex scenes available in graphic form, but only to those with the proper code; and to make Bibles with almost unlimited alternatives of translation, or with shuffled passages.

A phenomenon somewhat different from the new media convergence or from the transformation and increased dominance of the older media is the creation of networks of shared information and creative resources – the electronic bulletin boards, such as Internet with its 20 million and more users. If we combine with this technology fax capabilities, personal exchanges of audio and video cassettes, cellular phones, and low-powered television transmitters, we see the outlines of an alternative system, one that is often held up as a bastion of personal creativity, individual expression, and free exchange, and as a potential strength of democracy – the guarantor of the person against the collective system of corporate delivery. As McLuhan suggested many years ago,

> When the technology of a time is powerfully thrusting in one direction, wisdom may well call for a countervailing thrust. The implosion of electric energy in our century cannot be met by explosion or expansion, but it can be met by decentralism and the flexibility of multiple small centres.[4]

Futurist Alvin Toffler and many others have seen this kind of fracturing as an opportunity for new work patterns and lifestyles, as well as a safeguard against uniformity and Big Brotherism, and it may be argued that network-style media relations could offer a new and bright future to the arts, safeguarding individuality and localism while making possible a wide dissemination of the creative efforts of the (no longer) isolated individual.

It might be well to temper one's optimism about the possible results of arts networking, however, in the light of a few fundamental considerations. First, there is the question of how good the media are at presenting the arts, an issue that I address in the next chapter with respect to the main source, television. Then, too, there is cause to question how well the individualized personal networks will compete with the superpowered central delivery system. Will young people, for example, cut into their virtual reality trips, or their sitcom and rock-video watching time, in order to send and receive poems electronically? The passivity notably induced by television (*pace* McLuhan) may well be fatal in this respect. Furthermore, the issue of what may be freely presented on the new computer networks is by no means settled. Examples of censorship are already visible, and it is not clear that artistic freedom of expression will be guaranteed once computer networks include most members of society. Then, too, the effect of networking is inevitably to encourage a specialized, fractionalized audience; yes, browsing, like channel surfing, occurs, but this is hardly the way to create interest in new subjects or disciplines. The sheer volume of information in the favourite area tends to "eat up" the attention of the user, and we encounter the phenomenon of information overload; people stay in certain pockets to avoid the fatigue and confusion of exploration.[5]

In the past many children have been drawn to the arts through the indoctrination of a few "forced" attendances at performances, engineered by determined parents.[6] Yet parents exercise little control over their children's computer time. Today's children are far more sophisticated operators of technology than their parents, who generally end up bowing out in despair even if they have had some influence at the beginning. Will young people be drawn to the arts when there are so many competing sources of media satisfaction? It is doubtful.

Another question to ask is: what price will society pay for its almost obsessive attention to media development? Will government funding move away from the arts and culture in favour of promoting technology, on the (perhaps false) assumption that technological delivery systems are the wave of the future for these activities? Will the very existence of media gadgets and activities cause an inevitable decline in live-audience participation? And just who will the media audience be? Both American and Canadian society seem to be moving toward a greater split between the "information elite," who have access to the current hardware and software, and the "information deprived," who can afford a radio or television but hardly the expense of computers, updated programs, cable subscriptions, fax machines, and so on.[7] In the end it doesn't matter how receptive a network is to your interests if you can't afford to join it.

It is important for Canadians to realize that though there has been, and promises to be, a great deal of Canadian activity in media development of all kinds, the overwhelming financial control will continue to lie south of the border. The program content will remain overwhelmingly American, and the astounding new media – which obliterate borders and can hardly be controlled by government policies, or by decrees of the Canadian Radio-television and Telecommunications Commission – will only make it more likely that Canadian media users will be saturated with American-derived material and thus with American values.

To put this in perspective, some background is necessary. The brave new world that I have just outlined – which offers both creative possibilities and less pleasant outcomes – is novel only in its comprehensive nature and complexity. Canadian culture has faced equally perilous passages – if less complex technology – before. As the power of each of the modern media became visible, successive federal governments chose courses of action to deal with the issue of Canadian identity, which the new technology threatened to undermine. In the case of radio, these actions achieved excellent results; in film, after a disastrous start, much has been achieved; in the case of the most ubiquitous and potent of the new media, television, the record is poor.

The advent of radio meant the virtual abolition of the border between Canada and the United States; by the 1920s many Canadians were already tuning in to American programs, and local stations were increasingly controlled by American interests, but the establishment of the first coast-to-coast network (run by Canadian National Railways) made the idea of public ownership acceptable. The Aird Commission, appointed by Prime Minister William Lyon Mackenzie King in 1929, recommended the creation of a national broadcasting company; in 1932 R. B. Bennett's Conservative government acted on the Aird recommendations and passed the Canadian Radio Broadcasting Act.

The publicly owned Canadian Radio Broadcasting Commission, which, under new legislation (1936), became the CBC, began with eight stations and various privately owned affiliates. Within a few years, the CBC was powered up sufficiently to control Canadian airwaves; the development of indigenous programming took longer, but was remarkably successful. In the sphere of the arts, CBC Radio matured well, though it relied throughout its history on many imports, especially from the United States (Quebec, of course, had to create its own serials and popular features, and did so with great aplomb). The CBC did foster culture; drama in particular was excellent and ubiquitous, especially after the Second World War. Between 1944 and 1961, 3,000 original Canadian plays were produced in English Canada and, starting in the thirties, more than 1,500 in Quebec. These included plays by Lister Sinclair, Len Peterson, and Mavor Moore in English Canada, and by Jacques Godbout and Jacques Languir in the French-language series *Les Nouveautés dramatiques*.[8] Classical music, opera, critical arts commentary, and ideas programs also flourished on such venues as *CBC Wednesday Night*.

In the 1950s, however, when television was poised to become the reigning popular medium, CBC Radio began to lose touch with the new audience. Talk shows, continuous music, and frequent news broadcasts were coming on the scene; set-format shows were going out, and CBC listeners departed in great numbers. In the early 1970s, the corporation recovered, and found the excellent formula that has lasted virtually up to the present: elite, ad-free FM programming with a strong cultural and arts content, and a lively, talk-and-information-centred AM radio. Although further changes shuffled the deck a bit between AM and FM programming, this combination seemed to offer a strong presence of Canadian culture and arts on the airwaves, despite the continuous pressure of American content and the uninterrupted dominance of private broadcasting.

CBC Radio's historical commitment to arts programming, especially drama, and its eventual creation of its strong FM-stereo presence affirm the value of elite culture, a position derived from British, European, and American intellectual models. In such broadcasting, aesthetic culture is the norm, and the unashamed appeal is to educated listeners; advertisements are excluded, and the funding of new drama and music is seen as money culturally well spent.

Direct competition from strong and well-financed American enter-tainment sources, the Americanization of Canadian taste through films, and occasional uncertainties in dealing with social and technological changes made CBC Radio's passage to programming balance and cultur-al autonomy less than smooth, but the end result was admirable. (Ironically some of the most devoted CBC adherents were culture-deprived American radio listeners who lived close to the border.)

At the same time, in view of CBC Radio's long experience with the powerful American cultural challenge, and in light of the frequent con-cerns for Canadian identity expressed in successive government reports, one must be dumbfounded at the failure of successive federal governments to take the most obvious step to promote Canadian culture on television: i.e., to insist on the creation of an elite television channel equivalent to CBC FM-stereo. That no such CBC service has been established since television came to the fore in the early 1950s is really puzzling.

The actual CBC presence on television had some virtues in the mid-dlebrow sphere, but its commitment to serious culture was unfocused, spotty, and haphazard. Even the American television wasteland managed to achieve much more, at least at first: excellent new live drama, adapta-tions of classic works such as Conrad's *Heart of Darkness,* Orson Welles as Lear, original made-for-TV opera productions of rare works (such as Richard Strauss's original *Ariadne auf Naxos* and Leonard Bernstein's *Trouble in Tahiti*), innovative presentations of art, and discussions of cul-ture. Much of this programming was live, and it was about as exciting as serious culture can ever be on television.

What happened to the CBC? The Massey-Lévesque Commission in 1951 had reaffirmed the network's centrality to Canadian broadcasting and its importance as a cultural bastion, capable of controlling the environment in which it operated. This control began to be undermined when the Fowler Commission of 1955-56 recommended a separate regulatory agency; under John Diefenbaker's government, it was established in the form of the Board of Broadcast Governors, which had become by 1968 the Canadian Radio-television and Telecommunications Commission (CRTC). With the advent of cable television (which the CBC had no power to control), popular American programs made huge inroads into Canadian viewing habits and seriously damaged the advertising base of the CBC; at the same time, the CRTC was never successful in its attempt to regulate television so as to provide a rationally measurable quotient of "Canadian content" (the definition of which has proved elusive, to say the least). Other measures were more successful: specifying Canadian ownership of cable stations, free feeds from U.S. signals, and the recouping of some Canadian advertising revenues through tax policies. Yet while almost every study available, including those done by the CRTC, indicates that it is impossible to combine commercial television with cultural objectives, successive governments have failed to set up a consistently funded, elite public television channel (the so-called CBC-2), one that would have a national mandate and appropriate regional roots.

As recently as 1985, in the wake of the new Canadian cultural maturity, a respected Canadian television critic with a strong commitment to nationalism could advocate (among many other reformatory measures) the establishment of a CBC-2, with a mission of elite programming.[9] Ten years later, this kind of proposal still makes some sense, yet the situation has changed so much that doubts about its usefulness must arise. The Canadian public hardly seems ready to support huge expenditures on culture, even assuming they could be budgeted; at the same time, the CBC, far from being put on firm ground, has been undermined by cuts, threatened by unspecified "reforms," and bedevilled by administrative tinkering (not that change isn't needed). Most saliently of all, the shift into cable broadcasting and the arrival of even more radically new, and perhaps converging, technologies has made a CBC cultural channel less likely than ever.

The introduction of cable specialty channels (including arts, science, and lifestyle channels with significant Canadian content) might seem to have solved the problem of making our culture more visible on television; the idea of an elite CBC channel may even seem passé. Yet is it? When one examines the content of the new cable broadcasts (for example, on Bravo!), what turns up, by and large, is recycled material, most frequently foreign films; profiles of foreign artists and musicians; ballet films from the United States and England; Metropolitan and other opera broadcasts; as well as a great deal of old NFB and CBC material. After a year of hyping its devotion to the arts, Bravo! had to admit that its most popular show was *Dame Edna,* a late-night, transvestite comedy – a show of almost no artistic merit whatsoever. One sees almost no new creative work of any significance. Clearly the funding is not available, and the Canadian artists who might have been drawn into a CBC-2, had it been founded, say, in 1960 or 1970, or who might be available to cable, are no longer there. In fact, with the efflorescence of Canadian theatre in the sixties and seventies, many writers developed by CBC Radio moved over to Stratford and other live-theatre venues.

There is another slant on this situation, however. As of the mid-nineties, Canadian production companies (for example, CanWest Global,

Atlantis Films, Alliance Productions), thanks to the arrival of cable, were exporting some $300 million worth of Canadian-made programming around the world. The CRTC regulations that forced Canadian private broadcasters to buy Canadian material in the eighties acted as a seeding policy for many producers, who have gone on to exploit foreign markets (mostly using coproduction arrangements) not only in the United States and Britain but also in Eastern Europe, supplying them with rock videos, miniseries, and police dramas, not to mention Anne of Green Gables in all of her incarnations.[10]

The irony here is that Canadian-content regulations have partially ensured that our own enterprising companies are able to enter the international market and to supply dozens of countries with material that, though Canadian in origin, is, with a few notable exceptions, indistinguishable from the typical American product. Had the CBC developed an elite arts channel, financed by donations and cable fees, it could be producing serious art that would be in demand in narrow-market cultural services around the world. Such an enterprise would not only cover part of its production costs through revenue but would also be the means of marketing our distinctive elite culture around the world. This channel would be one way of ensuring that we don't lose out when the global network matures and solidifies.

If Canadian television has never really emerged as an arts medium, Canadian film, rebounding from a position of near hopelessness, has had notable successes. National film production started as early as 1897, and by 1913 the first successful feature, *Evangeline,* had been released, indicating the potential of an indigenous industry. American control of distribution in the twenties, however, paved the way for the destruction of Canadian initiative and, ignoring the example of many European countries, our federal government failed to take protectionist measures. Despite a few flares of activity, Canadian feature filmmaking had reached almost point zero by the time the NFB was founded in 1939.

The NFB began to train a generation of Canadian filmmakers, including Norman McLaren, Harry Rasky, Donald Brittain, Allan King, and Pierre Perrault, but the failure to achieve quotas in order to exact funding from the American imports meant that no substantial support appeared for new fiction features. In English Canada 20 years of sporadic activity followed, but the hoped-for national cinema failed to emerge; in Quebec, though attempts were made to play on the strengths of the local milieu and religion, a similar hit-and-miss approach failed to generate a viable industry.

The founding of the Canadian Film Development Corporation

(Telefilm Canada) in 1967 was a first step toward solving the problem of production costs. In the seventies, and even earlier in Quebec (the NFB had moved to Montreal in 1956), new filmmakers came on the scene. These included Don Shebib (*Goin' Down the Road*), David Cronenberg (*Crimes of the Future*), Ted Kotcheff (*The Apprenticeship of Duddy Kravitz*), Denys Arcand (*Réjeanne Padovani*), and Claude Jutras (*Mon Oncle Antoine*). These and others showed a formidable grasp of the Canadian landscape and psyche, and of social and generational conflicts. According to Peter Harcourt, "Canadian cinema is not fantasy cinema, or a cinema of escape. Repeatedly, it is an observational cinema. Characters are placed within their milieu and the films seem to ask why the characters behave as they do."[11] Where television never succeeded in achieving a projection of Canadian identity, cinema was often masterful.[12]

During the seventies and eighties, though several provincial funding agencies appeared, Telefilm Canada made what is generally considered a strategic mistake in focusing more and more on high-budget, Hollywood-style productions – few of which added anything of distinction to Canadian art. Many other films were created as tax shelters: low-budget horror, crime, and science fiction films, which added nothing of distinction to these genres. Fortunately this trend seems to have been reversed, and the problems of distribution have been addressed with more ingenuity and realism.

During the nineties, distinct and artistically focused Canadian films continue to be made, and they are attracting more and more international attention (for example, François Girard's *Thirty-two Short Films About Glenn Gould*, Atom Egoyan's *Exotica*, Robert Lepage's *Le Confessionnal*). Yet an increasingly sophisticated and profitable indigenous-production industry will continue to grow and to supply the genre films (fantasy, action, horror, science fiction) and the sentimental fiction films that play well in the lucrative world cable markets: few of these films will capture the spirit of Canadian culture or express profound values of any kind, though the profits generated may lead to better things.

In the realm of the mass media, Canadian arts and cultural institutions are being affected by developments that are taking place at such a rate, on such a scale, and by means of such large shifts of capital that they may be regarded as almost irresistible. Yet because many of the predicted developments will probably serve the arts dubiously or badly, it is important to keep in mind the possibilities of political action to transform or even obliterate some of these changes. Despite the fatalism of prophets such as Marshall McLuhan about the electronic revolution, and his mockery of those who question the authentic nature of some of the new media experiences, rearguard battles may have to be fought on various fronts. We should not assume too quickly that elegies must be spoken over the "arts as we knew them"; we should not, without a struggle, allow ourselves to be deprived by "progress" of some precious experiences, of values that give our lives real meaning and purpose, not to mention of pleasures that speak to the senses in the old ways.

One of these is the pleasure of reading books. In the sixties Canadian literature flourished; it fed, and was fed by, the new and consuming passion for national identity. Yet the development of a unique literary culture in Canada was undermined by the same disabilities that hindered the development of the creative arts in the mass media. Here was a small market adjacent to the American giant, enriched by the government's willingness to fund the artistic side, yet hampered by the reluctance of government to intervene to preserve an atmosphere in which new art could flourish. In 1972, when the real potency of Canadian literature had become apparent, and after Ryerson and Gage had been sold to American interests, and McClelland and Stewart threatened to go under, the federal government began giving aid to Canadian publishers.[13] In 1979 the Book Publishing Development Program was introduced, and a variety of grants, federal and provincial, funnelled through the Canada Council or provincial arts councils, continued through the nineties, though on a slowly diminishing level in relation to costs.

Some communications speculation would suggest that the print medium represents the past, that the end of the Gutenberg era is in sight. According to this kind of thinking, the arrival of the telecomputer, though it will naturally make use of print, will signal the end of the codex book as a separate entity. In fact, the old-fashioned book can be seen as a portable (and quite efficient) random-access reading machine. The arrival of the multimedia book, and the apparent decline of traditional reading skills and practices, may not signal the end at all, though they certainly indicate a shift in cultural perspective.

The Canadian literary boom of the sixties, seventies, and eighties coincided not only with the beginnings of the latest media revolution but also with a profound change in the structure of the publishing industry. The old family publishing houses were disappearing; many of them were bought up (cannibalized) by larger publishing groups, or by international conglomerates in search of new investments. The latter were often companies with no previous interest in communications, and as they sought to realize the cost of acquisitions, often financed by huge loans, expanded profit margins became a necessity. This, in turn, resulted in the "hyping" of the industry; the "world book" came on the scene, and there followed a frantic search for big sellers, accompanied inevitably by the death of midlist mainstream fiction.[14] Writers began to sign million-dollar contracts, and acquired, in the public eye, something of the glamour of baseball and hockey players. (The mad rush into creative writing courses was one result.) The specialized bookstore naturally began to disappear as well.[15]

In Canada small presses, which had been an important source of the new literature, were threatened by cutbacks in grants, and often by their own cliquish predilections, combined with an inability to innovate and find profit in the changing marketplace. Nonetheless, thanks to expert editors working with sophisticated computerized equipment, some of them were even turning out books that not only carried on the best traditions of Canadian literature but also earned large profits. Nino Ricci's *Lives of the Saints,* for example, was published by Cormorant Books, a small press indeed, run from a farmhouse in eastern Ontario. Partially thanks to the publicity generated by its Governor General's Literary Award (1990), it has sold more than 60,000 copies in Canada.

A grasp of even the general outlines of our recent past suggests a few conclusions about Canadian cultural development, the new technology, and the pitfalls and opportunities that may lie in the near future. First, nothing short of a planetary catastrophe is going to stop technological and media development; as Jacques Ellul and other analysts predicted, we now see a virtually autonomous process at work, one that has almost passed beyond the power of individuals, governments, and international organizations to control. Inevitability, however, does not confer morality or even utility on any process: not all aspects of these changes are good for society; not all are good for the best of culture as we know it. For one thing many – though not all – of the recent technological developments have favoured entertainment culture rather than aesthetic culture. Many "improvements" are justified on the grounds that they serve society – but whose society? The society of the masses ill prepared by education and longing for endless jolts of unthinking "entertainment"? The society of the teenager? Or the society of mature persons of whatever income level and origin striving to develop emotionally and to understand their lives and their world?

When we look at recent Canadian cultural history, we see that though Canadian aesthetic culture has sometimes been fostered by media developments, it is most often threatened and pushed into the background by the entertainment culture produced with such efficiency south of the border and broadcast to the world through the American media. Canadian local culture, unarguably, has often been overshadowed, sometimes obliterated, sometimes co-opted, by American mass culture. Not only Canada but also the world is held hostage to Michael Jackson, Disney's *Pocahontas,* and the Mighty Morphin Power Rangers, which, ironically, have a Canadian connection. (The Power Rangers' production company is controlled – very indirectly – by Power Corporation, Montreal.)

We have seen that Canadian serious culture, if not actually a product of federal government strategy (this is too simplistic), certainly owes its remarkable growth and survival in the post-Second World War period to the funding and nurturing provided by government sources on all levels. We have also seen that, having assisted in the creation of this vital culture, the federal government has sometimes been quite uncertain about how to develop it. Various crises have occurred, forcing government into action to protect radio, films, television, and book publishing from suffering fatal injury in the face of foreign competition, but the results have not always been satisfactory, mistakes have been made, and the argument for the value of serious culture to the survival of Canada has had to be made over and over again. As far as the arts and culture are concerned, most of our politicians and lawmakers seem to suffer from short-term memory loss.

In addition, though we know that culture has been excluded from the provisions of important international arrangements, specifically from the free trade negotiations with the United States, it will inevitably return as an issue should Canada begin to take further initiatives to market its elite cultural products around the world, which it certainly ought to do. Not only that, but new technologies (for example, direct-broadcast satellites) are literally ungrounded and borderless, and will be difficult to regulate by international agreements, even should we succeed in striking such agreements. The probability is that unless we take some strong action, such media will work against our cultural survival.

The tendency toward larger and more powerful media conglomerates also raises the question of whether Canada will act decisively enough to gain a place in the converging media of the future – not simply whether we can get a share of the technological action but also whether we can find a way to make our culture speak through the international media links that are coming into being all around us. Once again federal government action is imperative; without such intervention in this matter, we can expect very little interest in Canadian serious culture from media giants based in Los Angeles, Amsterdam, or Berlin.

If the worst Canadian nightmare happens, if Quebec finally separates, not only will the image of Canada be fractured beyond all recognition, but our national energies will be hopelessly sapped. Even an association between a new Quebec and a reformulated English Canada would compound, for both sides, the problems of protection of culture. English Canada, if shamefully lax in its appreciation of Quebec's cultural splendours, has at least, especially in educated circles, shown a sympathy for the enriching quality of the French fact. How long would Quebec individuality last when exposed to the full force of American mass culture, with which it has so far been able to carry on a discreet flirtation? How well would English Canadian culture flourish, having lost one of the elements that give it much of its distinct tone and tension? (In this respect two solitudes, though not ideal, may be safer than a separate peace.)

In the current rush toward the promised media wonderland of the next century, we should stop to ask a few questions:

1. Are we content to give up our national individuality, to accept the products of American mass culture, if it means that we get a share of the technological action?
2. Is it important that Canadian media groups are realizing huge profits, if they are delivering content that is indistinguishable from the content of American producers?
3. Even if we continue to value our serious culture and arts, can they survive in the mass media, which are inevitably geared to a broad audience and dominated by commercial interests?
4. How well does television (the dominant popular-entertainment medium) serve the arts, anyway?

Those of us who value the arts and serious culture, and who believe that Canada can hardly survive, in any vital sense, without them, may want to question the euphoria that seems to accompany our wild and seemingly uncontrolled ride toward international and converging media, toward the telecomputer in every living room, and toward virtual reality wrapped around everyone's head. Perhaps it is time to circumvent the technobabble that informs us that this media wrap is necessarily total, and that the appearance of the noosphere (the emerging global consciousness) is inseparable from futuristic hardware. Perhaps it is time to go in quest of the Grail (or Snark) of unmediated experience (which, some argue, is impossible and illusory). Is there nothing to be said, in this media-crazed world, for a live experience of the arts?

3 The Arts on Television, and Other Mind-numbing Pleasures

There is no more disturbing consequence of the electronic revolution than this: that the world as given to us through television seems natural and not bizarre.

— Neil Postman, *Amusing Ourselves to Death*

WHY DON'T THE ARTS WORK WELL on television? To answer this question, we must backtrack a little. Our media age comprises no more than an eye blink of human history. Discernibly human ancestors appeared on Earth between one and two million years ago; complex culture has been visible for 50,000 years, literacy for scarcely 5,000; the print revolution occurred 500 years ago; we have been media-saturated only since yesterday.

From oral to literate to media culture — a passage that has affected all aspects of human society, not least the arts. The oral-communication systems that nurtured the beginnings of human art and culture were rich and complex, but also immediate in that they were based on person-to-person communication; audiences could judge for themselves the authenticity of a given performance because they were directly in touch with a speaker or singer — with words, intonation, gestures. Simple songs and complex epics, ceremonial enactments, stories and philosophical debates — for thousands of years, all creative exchanges bore the guarantee of face-to-face experience. Then writing appeared, and the speaker began to disappear into the text. With the age of printing, ushering in the age of reading, huge gains are made in cultural storage, complexity, and extension of imagination, and a new kind of privacy emerges. But the existence of the text also notably transcends, or subverts, face-to-face experience. Writing, as Plato saw, could present the appearance of knowledge where there was none.[1]

A homely illustration may clarify this. If I am asked to *write* a recommendation for someone, I will have ample time to ponder my words, to decide what combination of them should produce the desired effect on behalf of the applicant. I may also consider the needs of the organization requesting the recommendation (as I understand them), and gauge my phrases accordingly. The temptation for me to be careful and to "dress up" the abilities of the applicant is great. Furthermore, I know that I must be careful about my negatives, for they will be stored and not pass away into thin air. The authorities requesting the recommendation will never see me sweating and straining to find the right words to convince them that the applicant is worthy; all they will get is (hopefully) a polished text. On the other hand, if someone *asks* me point-blank about the applicant, it will be much harder to dissemble. My facial expressions, posture, gestures, and voice rhythms will tell a story of their own. Face to face, I can disguise very little; therefore, I may be more honest, less guarded, and I may not hesitate to be a bit negative. Even on the telephone, my tone of voice may give something away.

If the passage from spoken to written culture already involves some loss of directness, a sacrificing of the personal to the impersonal medium, the recent development of the "media culture" is astonishing in its power to remove us from personal experience. Television is the most notorious example of this power, and is especially subversive because it simulates the face-to-face experience of an oral culture. Television flips us – with unparalleled realism, as it seems – into every kind of human situation: wars, political debates, sporting events, the birth of children, courtroom trials; a world unfolds and enfolds us. We get constant close-ups, intimacy of voice, and gestures: the illusion is given of an honest and direct projection of human experience. Yet – as critic after critic has pointed out – this projection is deceptive, a spurious mimicry of the older, oral culture. Boredom sets in easily; extensive viewing often results in irritation, seldom in the exhilaration felt by audiences at live events. A kind of hypnotic numbness, soporific and soothing, often follows long periods of television viewing. Television experience lacks all freshness: learning is not served; experience is trivialized. In addition, television is selective, and massively oversimplifies any event it attempts to encompass, as we have learned from endless political debates, discussion shows, feature interviews on complex issues, and news clips. But even in the simplest forms of entertainment, it creates distortions.[2]

Think how badly television conveys a baseball game: it is impossible to be engulfed by the roar of the crowd, to smell popcorn and sweating bodies, to be aware of sunlight and dust.[3] "The sense of the arena," which links all mass sporting events to the ancient past, is absent. And the camera shows us only the endpoints and crises of the game's action; relentlessly following the ball, we lose the sense of panorama, and the freedom to watch the game in our own way is taken away from us. We cannot study the dugouts or the shifts of the outfielders. The camera sees what it is designed to see, what the producer or technical director wants it to see. The *process* of the game eludes us.

The first time I saw a baseball game on television, the screen was the size of a large wooden matchbox; the figures were minuscule, blurred black-and-white ghosts; the single camera was rigidly fixed at a spot behind the plate, and only covered a small patch of infield. The ball was nearly invisible, and the outfielders might as well have been in Mongolia. To me the miracle was simply that I could see, in a crude way, some of the things I knew only as verbal signals (from the radio). Yet in the fullness of my imagination (I hadn't yet been to a real ball game), and on the basis of my sandlot playing, I *knew* the game in a way that television could never reveal to me.

And still cannot – for though the sharpness and range of vision have been greatly improved, and colour has brought a sense of realism, as I watch, my sense of the game is still diminished by the limitations of the medium. I have no freedom to connect or construct the events in my own way; the focus is already decided for me. I am presented with what amounts to a "staged" event, an impersonal and carefully contrived "show," while the constant breaks for advertisements take me away from the game altogether. In the light of these limitations, the improvements in technological means achieved since my childhood seem merely distracting.

Still worse, they now distort the "live" experience of major league baseball. To attend a game in a modern domed stadium is to be assaulted with media hype. And the more you pay the worse it is. In the VIP boxes, for example, you hang high above a green baize of artificial turf, with the stadium's giant screens flashing replays, advertisements, messages, close-ups of the audience – the ultimate in video game graphics. These images never let up, nor do the sound effects; meanwhile, giant-screen television sets are situated nearby, and smaller ones hang within reach. These visual and audio stimuli make it extremely difficult to concentrate on the "real" action – which, of course, may not matter to most VIP patrons.

I have used the example of baseball because the action of the game, unlike that of hockey or basketball, unfolds in plays of limited duration, followed by pauses, while, unlike both hockey and football, body contact is relatively rare, enabling the spectator to focus analytically on the central action. Baseball should be an ideal television spectacle, yet it is not; and the arts are even less so, for a variety of reasons.

Because the arts are complex and multifaceted, and are seldom broadcast in real time, television has little power to convey them. If the "feel" of baseball comes across poorly on television, the spirit of the arts is almost wholly lost. The camera, despite its power of close-up, distorts, while the editing process takes us far from the complexity of the live arts event. Television allows, almost demands, the manipulation of reality, but does little to enhance the power of art to communicate truth.

The worst case is probably the televising of classical chamber or orchestral music, a practice that is not only visually tedious but also distracting for the serious listener. The camera moves around, picks up, shall we say, a clarinet player who has a brief solo, but this close-up may annoy the listener who is trying to catch some subtle concurrent touch in the string section. As for the sight of back-desk personnel, who often seem about to yawn, of grimacing, posturing soloists, or of sweating conductors – what does it add to the music? Even the promise of vastly improved sound systems seems insufficient to justify the televising of most classical music performances.

To combat these obvious visual limitations, however, we now have classical versions of rock music videos. We hear an orchestra bashing out a Bartok hungarian dance while the camera shows us actors performing strange rituals in a cornfield, or we listen to Handel concerti grossi while endless shots of (surprise!) baroque palaces and ornate formal gardens flash by. While the Handel visuals may be merely tedious, the addition of "a dumb show" to music can be very annoying to the listener who does not want his or her treasured musical experiences polluted with extraneous associations, however "creative." Even worse, the alert viewer will have noticed the tedious repetitions of performances by "the three tenors," who, as time passes (and their time *is* nearly past), desperately seek more and more involvement with pop artists in order to buttress their sagging invention and their increasingly bankrupt repertory of visual distractions and "over the top" musical numbers.

As for complete opera performances, thanks to the built-in dramatic component, these fare better on television, yet they remain very unsatisfactory in fundamental ways. Once again the camera is largely to blame, but there are other problems. Opera began as and remains a baroque form, which means that it is generally conceived as a spectacle; operas move at a leisurely pace; they are static and hierarchical in nature, and laden with nonrealistic conventions (even in the case of the *verismo* style of Puccini and others). These aspects conflict strongly with television's pseudo-realism, as with its penchant for the close-up and the quick cut. Watching an opera on television is almost painful – the camera wants to go faster than the show allows. Add to this problem the lack of space around the figures, the often stiff acting, the threat of the imminent disgorging of the tenor's or soprano's larynx – these undermine the beguiling illusionism and destroy the theatrical excitement that one often experiences at a live performance of opera.

Some of the same limitations apply to dance on TV. But whereas opera moves too slowly to be effective on television, dance moves too fast and presents far too many subtleties of movement and gesture. The lack of depth of field is also daunting. Like opera, dance is not meant to be seen close up, and no matter how ingenious the camera movements, the thrilling sense of bodies making meaningful patterns in space is lost.

If classical music and dance fare poorly on television, then what of art – traditional painting and sculpture? How do they survive the medium? In fact, television seems hardly to have served the visual arts at all. To be sure, over the years certain expensively produced and well-thought-out shows have made their mark, namely Kenneth Clark's *Civilization,* as well as Robert Hughes's *The Shock of the New* and Michael Wood's *Art of the Western World.* Unfortunately a pattern of presentation evolved in these shows, which by now has almost become a production cliché. This involves an articulate and highly visible narrator who smoothly carries us from one artwork to the next, leaping over barriers of time and distance. There are many on-location shots, editing that leaves hardly a breath for reflection, and a strong central thesis that gives each presentation the somewhat spurious unity of a postgraduate thesis. This is not a good way to discover art. (Sister Wendy, who manages to break some of the clichés, is the exception that proves the rule.)

As for the televising of actual art shows, this is almost never attempted in North America. What we do see occasionally are films on art made for educational purposes, the kind of thing that every large gallery stockpiles and uses with lectures or exhibitions.[4] Although sometimes used as "filler," or to meet legislated commitments, art is curiously rare on the visual medium of television. Yet the opportunities for experimentation and ingenuity exist. American television once featured a program called *What in the World?* in which three anthropologists attempted to identify objects chosen to baffle them from all the world's cultures: this kind of idea, one would think, would have inspired many variants.

Although colour instability and, once again, the focal nature of the camera put severe limits on the completeness of any television experience of painting and sculpture, the more overriding negative is probably the characteristic TV fear of the static. When we do see art on television, it is through the eye of an endlessly moving camera, through restless pans and dissolves that might almost symbolize the inability of our culture to achieve the fixed concentration required to come to terms with great works of visual art.

Clearly drama is the art form that suits television the best, and that TV has served better than any other. In the popular vein, many effective, even literate, series have emerged, ranging from often inspired sitcoms (*All in the Family* or *M*A*S*H*) to recastings of classic novels and stage works. In the so-called golden age of American television (from just after the Second World War until about 1960), the 52-minute live theatrical performance on series such as *Kraft Television Theater* and *Studio One* gave hope for a new form of media theatre, one that has never been truly realized.[5] This breakthrough seems to have occurred because pioneering American TV writers and dramatists, like some of the first CBC dramatists, both French and English, sensed that television's strongest suit, in a theatrical sense, lies in the depiction of ordinary people living ordinary lives. Not kitchen-sink theatre but theatre for the living room, in a low-key, intimate vein: genre theatre.

Yet if, in the name of supporting aesthetic culture, the more elegant and formal arts (opera, ballet) are occasionally broadcast and paid for, serious drama, which ought to be ubiquitous on television, has greatly shrunk in significance. This is because the commercial climate of the medium has virtually destroyed any possibility of a living television theatre. Thus, the few attempts in recent decades at running quality drama on both American and Canadian television (for example, the *Festival* and *Folio* series, Atlantis Films' Canadian short story series, and Robert De Niro's *Tribeca*) have fallen under the gun of production costs. Although American sitcoms can cost up to $1 million an hour to produce, commercial sponsors can be counted on to buy into them, whereas such sponsors would run away from drama appealing to a smaller audience and dealing in controversial or bold ways with serious issues. What we do get are occasional special presentations on public broadcasting or arts channels, and even this fare tends to be film-derived and repetitious. No new serious dramatists are being recruited by North American TV; there is no mass audience, it is argued, for serious drama.

Significantly, more than any of the other arts just mentioned, drama is capable of offering a direct threat to the assumptions of a complacent public, more capable of stirring up trouble, of offending conventional assumptions, of challenging pressure groups and minorities, who may have the ear of legislators, or the middle classes, who are the target of the advertisers. In a healthy society, one in which truth and beauty counted for something, one in which the government wished to ensure that its citizens were well informed, alert, and thinking persons, a national-television theatre series (under one aegis, but playing regional material in various regions and in the two languages) would be a first priority. The best playwrights would be encouraged to write for such a series, and frequent competitions would enlist fresh talent. The decentralization of artistic juries would ensure that local work not be overlooked, and would counter potential bureaucratization. Extensive publicity would seek to make such theatre an eagerly anticipated collective experience (countering the fractionalizing of audiences I referred to earlier, which is not in every case a good thing). The goal might be to elevate such programming to iconographic status ("Theatre Night in Canada," a high-culture riposte to *Hockey Night in Canada,* which also combines regional programming under a national aegis). Such a plan, had it been initiated in the sixties or seventies, might have achieved far more for Canadian culture than, for example, the building of the National Arts Centre in Ottawa, which is neither national, nor artistically vital, nor a centre.

Perhaps it is now too late for such a dream of government-funded, quality television drama. Commercialization has gone so far, fractioning of audience is so advanced, that nothing that breaks the conventional mould can be expected to appeal to today's audiences. Lulled into passivity, stupefied by decades of sitcoms and soap operas, betrayed by successive governments that have refused to legislate content or quality, let down by our educational systems, most Canadians are manifestly incapable of responding to anything but the most blatantly mindless fare.

There are, indeed, good reasons (as I have been suggesting all along) for abandoning hope for the arts on television and for encouraging all levels of government to support live theatre, live music, live dance, right across Canada. Neil Postman makes the point that the medium itself is virtually immune to quality; he argues – only half facetiously – that those who seek to "improve" TV by upgrading its level of content only *lower* the level of the valuable material they force upon it. TV is incorrigibly trivializing. And it is certainly true that the media experience of art, in particular the television experience of art, is paltry when compared with the live experience. This is because the live experience is *unframed* and *self-directed, eventful, historical,* and *communal.*

It is unframed and self-directed in the sense that, as a member of a live audience, I have the power to experience any given artistic event from my own centre, to take in the overall atmosphere, and to choose (up to a point) my particular mode of encountering the event. We can select our seats in a theatre or concert hall, fix our attention on particular details, focus on the whole or a particular part of a performance. We can look at one picture at an exhibition, at one installation or many. We can go "cold" to an event or read up on it in advance, sometimes meet the artist, size up the audience, and talk over the experience with friends.

Experiencing arts events in this way wakes us up, urges us into activity, though we can withdraw and take a meditative stance if we wish: what is important is that we are personally engaged. The experience is not preset, distorted by someone else's agenda, or cut short where we don't wish it to be.[6]

Live experience is eventful in the sense that accidents may happen. If the tenor adds a high C in a Verdi aria, or a dancer improvises brilliantly in *Swan Lake,* we are charmed; if the horn player muffs a solo in Strauss's *Don Juan,* or Hamlet or Hedda Gabler drops a line, we wince, but are not stuck with hearing it forever. Such accidents or improvisations betoken our freedom, and recall the reality of the moment and our participation as real people in a unique event.

By contrast, prerecorded music is often so artificially reconstructed that it bears no resemblance to a coherent performance. In one Chicago Symphony recording, over 200 splices were necessary to correct errors in a 20-minute piece.[7] Toward the end of this chapter, I will deal briefly with Glenn Gould, who – it is well-known – lauded this kind of artifice, this technological control. But is it really music-making?

Everyone who goes to arts events has had the delightful experience of having an unexpected thrill in a situation that no one bothered to record, because it promised nothing special in advance. I once attended a Mahler and Bruckner concert in, of all places, Cornwall, Ontario. The National Youth Orchestra was led by Georg Tintner, and though I knew of Tintner's interest in Bruckner, his somewhat tepid and unsuccessful recordings had not prepared me for what took place. In fact, the concert was transporting. I sat astonished and thrilled. Later, however, I began to doubt. Had I been starved so long for a live performance of this music that I had greatly overrated what I heard? Fortunately I met a friend afterward, an experienced musician and Mahler addict, who confirmed that my pleasure had been far from merely subjective. This is the kind of unique moment, a wonderful treat, unexpected and unprogrammed, that a live performance can open up.

Such moments, in fact, become *historical*. It means more to me that I heard Sir William Walton conduct his First Symphony at the Proms in London, or Sir Thomas Beecham conduct Mozart and Strauss, than that I can procure taped or filmed versions of these events. Such experiences not only become precious strands of complex personal memories but also place us historically as members of our society, as participants in the life of our time. They are not nonevents, even when they fail to carry us to the heights; they enrich our lives and give us a sense of possibility and diversity, confirming the open quality of our experience.

Apart from some momentous news events (the Oswald assassination, Kennedy's funeral, the first moon landing), almost nothing we take in on television, or see on a computer screen, enters us in the sense of becoming part of our life experience. As viewers or even as manipulators of machinery with preset programs, we remain passive; we engage in no process. Why is it that all the TV presentations we recall tend to run together in an uneasy blur of memory? Clearly it is because they are associated with no real texture of event in our lives, because they take place in a limbo of nontime and nonevent. This litter of "entertainment" piled up in our memories, unmemorable and diffuse, makes a mockery of television's time obsession, of the careful scheduling of its programs, of its supposed ability to recapitulate the oral directness and power of arts experience at its most primal.

Television's final failure as an arts medium, however, is that it is not communal, that it cannot produce the particular joy, the sustained energy and appreciation, felt by an audience at a live event. At a well-attended exhibition, you can share the active responses of those drifting multitudes of strangers around you. Even crowding doesn't matter, for as René Dubos points out, modern urban crowding is obnoxious not so much because of high population density but because of the great amount of technology that each inhabitant commands and can force on others.[8] In a gallery, or at a concert hall, where technology wielding is restricted, and where everyone is eager to experience the event in question, a crowd can be pleasant. Despite numbers, at the best moments of an orchestral concert or a live opera, an audience gains the power to escape the earthbound; the narrow ego of the individual is transcended, and we get precisely the sense of human unity that McLuhanism perversely ascribes to the media experience. And the audience's expressed delight, the applause at the end, is not to be confused (*pace* Gould) either with the appreciation of sheer athletics or with a mindless yielding to the collective.

On the contrary we applaud because we have been moved, touched emotionally. We respond at the same moment in the same place, and find that our individual joy is magnified, that it echoes back to us from other souls (because that is what they are at that moment: *souls,* not mind-body machines).[9] At such a moment we achieve a unique feeling of unanimity. This is because we have been privileged witnesses to the skill of the performers in revealing the beauty and truth of the work. We were *there.*

I understand that there is pleasure and value in solitary, singular experience with art; it is clear that the reproduction of music and art, making it possible to have an experience alone, or at one's leisure, is valuable. But surely nothing we get from the media – radio, television, books, CDs – can remotely match the richness of the live experience of art shared with others.

True, television especially may sometimes serve to give the arts a visibility in mass life. I insist, however, that to rely exclusively on television, or other media, for our artistic pleasures is to guarantee that what we experience will be limited, that we will certainly lose freedom, excitement, and authenticity in doing so. What's more, the obliteration of live performances by the mass media, tapes, videos, and audio recordings would be a cultural tragedy of huge dimensions. This truth has been somewhat obscured by the magnificent obfuscations of those two singular Canadian geniuses, Marshall McLuhan and Glenn Gould.

Both McLuhan, the thinker as performer and guru, and Gould, the performer as thinker and anchorite, came to wear an almost religious aura (slightly different in each case), and both derived from traditions that seem far removed from the mathematically based technology and science that underlie all the media. McLuhan was a professor of English, with his roots in the study of Renaissance literature, and with a special interest in literary modernism, in the writings of Ezra Pound, T. S. Eliot, and Wyndham Lewis. Gould schooled himself in the stylistic world of Bach, in the modernism of Schoenberg, and in the so-called second Viennese school. McLuhan, who declared that "the job of the artist is to keep people tuned to the present," became an elusive and provocative thinker whose analysis of the impact of communications technology veered away from logical argument and took the form of the sutra, of brief enigmatic deliverances upon the mysteries of the media.[10]

McLuhan at his most characteristic engaged in an intellectual tightrope walk, critiquing the media (especially television) in an original and seemingly objective fashion, while promoting a brave new world where the medium is the message, where technology as the physical extension of the human percipient determines the content of human creativity. Although disclaiming ideological adherence to the phenomenon of commercial television, and "exposing" the advertising industry, McLuhan tacitly justified the manipulation of the audience (by political groups or advertisers) in the name of a spurious kind of interactionism (television engages the body). McLuhan's Janus-like ideology, while setting the tone for all euphoric and salvationist advocates of new media, was also clearly historicist. That is, it argued that because the phenomenon (of the new media) is here, and came about as part of comprehensible historical changes, it must be good and necessary.

Humankind, McLuhan suggested, has extended its nervous system via technology; the sheer speed of information processing makes it possible to gather all history, all thought, into the present. Old-fashioned ways of knowing had to give way to "pattern recognition"; we were like the Norwegian fisherman in "A Descent into the Maelstrom," the famous story by Poe, threatened by a whirlpool, but if we understood the fluctuations of the whole, the patterns, we could avoid destruction.

While McLuhan wrote provocatively about almost everything he touched on, the maelstrom of his thinking process offers little possibility of clarity. For example, though he noted endless examples of media distortions of truth and beauty, he produced no clear and useful analysis of this insidious power, and never dealt forcefully with television's banality, its way of undermining human energy and creativity and of misrepresenting almost every aspect of our existence, including the arts. Instead, he left the door open for naive predictions about how television would transform us all for the better, lending support by his aphoristic inconclusiveness to some absurd notions, such as the thought that television could be a "new spiritual medium," a forecast realized in grim, ironic form in the mounting wave of fundamentalist and other religious claptrap that threatens to pollute the channels.

McLuhan, as an orthodox Roman Catholic, was a little wary of the writings of Teilhard de Chardin, which were banned by the church. However, the Jesuit thinker's notion of "planetary consciousness," his idea of the movement toward God as the omega point or end of history (espoused in a bleaker, but more humanistic, form by the great science fiction writer, Olaf Stapledon), influenced McLuhan, who became the questing knight of media thought, looking for the saving grail among the rubbish of television advertising, sitcoms, 30-second clips, and idle chatter that passes for entertainment and information.

Glenn Gould, by contrast, a great pianist and a sensitive, complex thinker, horrified by the inadequacies, distortions, and absurdities of the competitive world of the concert hall, gave up the quest (i.e., live performances) and retreated in 1964 into a world of privileged studio isolation, much to the delight (and profit) of the CBC and the record companies. "By far the most important electronic contribution to the arts is the creation of a new and paradoxical condition of privacy," Gould declared.[11] The paradox lay in the fact that while the greatest possible audience could enjoy the experience, each listener was supposedly freed from the captivity and automatonlike state that Gould saw as the condition of the concert audience (whose future demise he also predicted).

Gould embraced McLuhan's media extensions of consciousness, but in the name of meditation: "the purpose of art is not the release of a momentary ejection of adrenaline but is, rather, the gradual lifelong construction of a state of wonder and serenity."[12] It was as if he had ascended – or wished to ascend – into that very media heaven that McLuhan had prophesied. (If there is ever a Unified World Christian Church, and a Canadian is elected pontiff, if he is not called Pope Marshall I, he would clearly have to style himself Pope Glenn I.).

An anchorite in the heart of urban Toronto, an eccentric and a "personality," whose highest value was an almost mystical "self-emptying," Gould saw the studio as a blessed kind of laboratory in which he could reassemble each element of a performance until it shone with a transcendental perfection that bore the illusion of spontaneity.[13] His nervous temperament, his introversion, what could be taken as his flight from the physical (the source of some of his strengths as a thinker and artist), also led him to extreme positions. Do the media really offer the listener a chance of greater creative participation in a work than a live performance? Is heartfelt applause at the end of a splendid concert performance really the tribute of an audience of robots? Has the system of recording cured the ills of the concert hall, or has it not added a few of its own? (Such as memorializing inadequate performances by young artists who are forced by the system of media competition to record works before they are ready.) As for musical contests and their evils, it seems that their purpose now is to win recording contracts for young artists so that they can make the 99th version of the Tchaikovsky or a Rachmaninoff piano concerto, or a new set of The Goldberg Variations to compete with Gould's![14]

Pointing out contradictions and inadequacies in McLuhan's and Gould's theorizing, however, has never seemed a useful task. For both thinkers, artfully interpreting the media in quasi-religious terms, succeeded in mythologizing their own missions and in passing beyond arguments (Marxist, liberal, or pragmatic) directed at their exaggerations.

This mythological screen, however, does not quite hide the absurdities evident in the speculations of even an informed and learned contemporary exponent of McLuhan's theories. Derrick de Kerckhove, director of the McLuhan Program in Culture and Technology at the University of Toronto, rhapsodizes about the possibilities of "virtual reality" as a creative medium, and, following McLuhan, makes excellent points about the desire of Western society to transcend the body. He also admits that the old media will remain as alternative vehicles of communication, even though he argues that the future technological arts will open wonderful new channels of experience, that they will once again get the spectator into the centre of the artwork – that the Symbolist dream of synaesthesia (the concurrent response of two or more of the five senses to a stimulus), or a new kind of multisensory traversal of an aesthetic program, will be possible.[15]

Yet to suggest that the narcissistic "closed loop" of a virtual reality system returns us in some way to the ancient experience of preliterate cultures is an idea that only a professor at an institute of communications named after McLuhan could take seriously. If you want to simulate the experience of preliterate culture, to "integrate the whole field of your experience," I suggest a canoe trip on a very quiet lake during the Canadian summer. Let yourself float along, feel the breeze touch your hands and forehead, quietly take in the dazzle of light on the water, drift with the slow clouds, let your mind empty and your body begin to move to the rhythms of the waves, be alert to the movement and buzz of the dragonflies, the fast-swirling waterbugs, the leaping fish, feel the stirring of the greenery on the near shore, smell the dark, rich mud of the shallows. After a while you will be transported, if not to a preliterate world, at least to an integrated and living world beyond the reach of any technological system. You will have integrated the whole field of your experience in an ancient and powerful way, and there will be nothing narcissistic about it, nothing of the modern ego projection and machine dependency. You will certainly not be part of a closed loop, and therefore your experience will be "real" in a way that exposes "virtual reality" as the very unvirtuous reality that it is (the political implications of this technology are particularly frightening).[16]

The giveaway, I think, pointing up the weaknesses of the de Kerckhove stance is his attitude to television. McLuhan's absurd notion that T V viewing is an "active" neuromuscular experience is maintained by his disciple. "Nothing happens in your head when you watch," de Kerckhove tells us (quite right, for the most part, given T V 's content) – but your body is completely involved.[17] An odd assertion, surely, because the reaction of most viewers is unease after much watching, the desire to get out and move the body, just to "do something," to activate oneself after the enforced passivity and induced lethargy – mental *and* physical – of viewing. And to suggest that channel surfing constitutes a viewer's "editing" of the media content, his or her entry into a kind of virtual reality (instead of being the nervous tic, or at best the family-couch power trip, that it is for most serious flippers), is surely the height of nonsense.

Let us be brutally accurate and reflect the real (if mostly unacknowledged) experience of most viewers. Television viewing is *never* a creative act; it is a lethargy-inducing habit, which removes us from active learning and from the body. The main social usefulness of television – to give it its due – has been to deparochialize the outlook of the average person, who cannot live any longer with quite the same narrow sense of the world that was possible once upon a time, whether in rural Saskatchewan or urban Chicago. Television creates a kind of median consciousness; it slightly raises the awareness level of the deprived, while lowering that of the more fortunately endowed. Television is a pseudo-companion; it gives one the illusion of not being alone. For this reason it serves the elderly in nursing homes, where, one notices, TVs are ubiquitous, yet where no one seems to be actively watching. But TV is also a sphere of idolatry – it creates false idols, blows up the images of ordinary and mediocre people, inflates ordinary and mediocre thoughts and gives them an apparent significance. It conveys no important human experience accurately and well, offering instead a précis of reality. It cannot render the birth of a child from a mother's perspective, or even through the eyes of a father looking on; it gives no sense of the world in which we live and on which we are dependent; it is hopelessly superficial at conveying ideas and even information.

If I have become fixated on television, the reader will realize why. First, it is the medium we all accept most unconsciously, hardly realizing its presence at all – or its distortions. And second, precisely for that reason, I am using television as a metaphor of what happens when the modern media achieve a complete "wrap" around our experience. If this wrap occurs in the case of our traditional arts experiences, if the technological side intrudes too much upon our theatres, books, operas, ballets, poetry readings, if it threatens to consume them, our culture is in trouble indeed.

Television is *not* a global village, recorded music cannot replace live music, the experience of nature is not adequately mediated by the media, and the direct experience of art and nature will never be made obsolete, even by the wildest reaches of the most futuristic communications technology. If the media have added huge possibilities to arts experience, and introduced many practical advantages (though certainly not McLuhan's transcendental moments) for both performers and audiences, these same media (television, radio, recordings of all kinds) can nonetheless be seen to embody limitations in communication that are intrinsic, and to raise social and political problems that are daunting. We are not heading yet toward media utopia or nirvana. The live performance must still be the first consideration of a healthy artistic culture.

4 Arts or Entertainment: The Crisis of Quality

*Think of Batman or Madonna and try to find yourself a place on
the globe where you are not destined to be accompanied by the
ocean of hype that our screens and newspapers pour out, not least
here in Toronto, where our media can compete with anyone in tout-
ing and trumpeting the latest Hollywood genius.*
— Allan Gotlieb, "Canada in the 1990s: The Canadian
Cultural Challenge"

THE MASS MEDIA are central to any discussion of the future of the
arts and culture in Canada. They deliver "entertainment," usually
meaning large injections of popular culture, most of which has an
American origin and bias. This "entertainment culture" coexists with aesthetic culture and occupies the majority, while aesthetic culture occupies
the minority. Television, far more than religion, is the contemporary "opium
of the masses," but if we also look at radio, films, recordings, and books, we
see the extent to which the public's consumption of culture is connected
with the most easily assimilable, lowest-common-denominator values and
modes of expression. Entertainment culture is marketed in conjunction
with the consumerism that is an integral part of capitalism. And some of the
eerier aspects of this "culture" (Madonna, the trial of O. J. Simpson, *Unsolved
Mysteries*) point to a decadent or late phase of Western society, to a "postmodern" era in which sophistication and cynicism combine in a shameless
application of the most outrageous and outré means of filling us with ideas,
emotions, and images that are vapid, degrading, sentimental, or simplistic.

At this point I can almost hear the reader's protest – I can imagine a
simmering of outrage: "Oh, no, not another tirade in the name of so-
called superior or high culture. What's wrong with mass culture, anyway?
What's wrong with entertainment for its own sake? What about the
Rolling Stones and Barbra Streisand and *The Lion King* and *Frasier* –

don't we exercise discrimination among the products of mass entertainment, too?" We do, of course, and it is amazing how quality sometimes triumphs amid conditions that seem to encourage only the worst. Nonetheless, in the discussion of cultural levels and values, a few important points often escape us, and I want to deal with them here.

First, we are experiencing – and will experience even more completely in the future – a situation in which the local roots of popular culture are being obliterated.[1] We are heading for a universal entertainment culture, one that transcends national boundaries and more and more destroys the possibility of individuality and local self-expression.[2] Second, most of the world's entertainment culture promises to be of American origin, or to imitate American-style products. Third, this entertainment culture promotes certain values and attitudes, some of which are intimately related to American ideals, presumptions, national paradigms, and myths.[3] Fourth, this homogenous entertainment culture – though far from "evil" – has negative effects on society. It fosters collective behaviour and thinking, promotes the notion that anything that doesn't realize a profit is valueless, frames reality in simplistic terms, introduces and maintains a confusion between popularity and quality, reduces the question of taste to a simple gut reaction, or to knowing what's "with it" or "in," and frequently denigrates precise language and discipline in favour of violent communication and "impact." At its worst it also degrades and mocks the very people who feed on it – the Dick Assmans, the weepy or defiant victims who bare all to Oprah Winfrey, the quiz-show goonies (you and me with dunce caps).

As a small country precariously placed next to the world's entertainment giant, Canada is particularly vulnerable to the "Coca-Cola conspiracy," to the almost routine subversion of its cultural identity by the smoothly fashioned products of American mass culture. For Canadians involved in popular entertainment, one answer has been to join the winning side, to move where the action is, to accept reality – choose your metaphor – and either migrate south or produce material that is so Americanized as to be indistinguishable from the original. And the question has been raised: is this clever opportunism, or capitulation? Nationalists argue that even on the level of entertainment culture, Canadians would be better served by specifically Canadian material, that *The King of Kensington* or even *The Beachcombers* must be preferable to American shows of the same quality, that Gordon Lightfoot, who has remained basically Canadian, is culturally of more value than William Shatner, who became an American icon. Internationalists argue that to promote and support Canadian popular entertainment is often to bankroll mediocrity, that

Canadians "don't want" local material unless it is as good as the American competition (and sometimes not even then), and that "realism" and "freedom of expression" in the popular arts are more important than nationalist cultural agendas.

While entertainers should be able to go where they wish and present whatever they choose, one part of the nationalist argument seems to make some sense. When the influx of foreign material is controlled, local material can appear to fill the vacuum. The classic example is the comic book caper of 1941-46, which has become a prime example for nationalists of the power of government to promote Canadian production of culture by simply prohibiting the competition.[4] In 1941 the government of Mackenzie King decided to include comic books among the "nonessential" items that would be banned from importation during the war crisis. Both the comics and the printing mats were not allowed to be shipped across the border. As a direct result, the Canadian comic book industry was born. It flourished, though only for a few years, producing black-and-white ("Canadian white") strips, and giving birth to such authentic Canadian images as Johnny Canuck and Nelvana of the Northern Lights.

Johnny Canuck, according to his creator Leo Bachle, was supposed to "typify the Canadian character" and be "Canada's answer to Nazi oppression," while Nelvana, perhaps based on Inuit legend, was a beautiful sub-Arctic superwoman descended from a long line of powerful female figures, rulers of the lost worlds of the pulps, a "White Goddess" type first created by H. Rider Haggard in his Victorian adventure story *She*.

In 1946, when the import ban was lifted, the Canadian comics disappeared (not only the ones mentioned but almost all the indigenous comics in both English and French Canada), and the cross-border exchange shifted to the general question of the harmful effect of comics on children. To guard against these supposed effects, Louis St. Laurent's government instituted a ban on certain American comics, which encouraged U.S. crusaders in their battle for a national cleanup, and resulted, ultimately, in the American Comics Code Authority of 1954.

This fleeting – and seemingly insignificant – bit of Canada's cultural history has, for many nationalist commentators, taken on almost the force of a parable, and one can understand why. It seems, on the surface, a textbook (or comic book) example of how Canadian culture might flourish if only government would act to control or ban the competing cultural material from the United States. In that brief span of years, Canada seems to have enjoyed freedom from the American popular-culture industry, something never achieved in any other medium. The Canadian war comics, poorer in quality in many ways than the American, expressed – it is argued – something intrinsically Canadian, and their demise seems yet another example of the imperialistic reach of the American entertainment industry, which has the power to obliterate any competing industry not protected by government action.

So the argument goes, and it is certainly plausible, though one-sided. Admittedly the ironies are huge. The Canadian government (rather inadvertently) not only succeeded in promoting a fleeting life for Canadian content in comics (something it was slow to do in film and radio) but also, by withdrawing its support, destroyed what it had created. To cap it all, Canadian legislation helped to foster a more puritanical and censorious attitude south of the border, probably resulting in a lowering of standards – and certainly limiting freedom of expression – in the American industry. Protectionism appeared as a substitute for quality; the Canadian material simply couldn't survive without it, for American comics were not only better produced but also seemed to have some innate appeal that Canadians could hardly resist. Superman (co-created by a Canadian!), Batman, and Spider-Man – these became world-famous figures. The Green Hornet, the Blue Beetle, The Flash, Captain Marvel, and Wonder Woman were only slightly less well-known. One might cynically ask: why should Canadians prefer a provincial nobody such as Johnny Canuck when they could choose from among such a dazzling crew? Even when the Johnny Canuck idea was revived and given a quality format in the Captain Canuck comics of the 1970s, it only survived briefly. Neither it nor the more intriguing Cerebus the Aardvark has lasted, despite the strong post-sixties commitment of Canadians to their own cultural artifacts.

In order to understand this situation a little better and to get to the heart of the central issues confronting Canadian culture, whether popular or aesthetic, some background is necessary. Some of what we call popular culture, all over the world, could be traced, through many of its manifestations, to a lively and individual local or folk culture. American jazz, for example, moved from its roots in the black experience in the South to become, sometimes in diluted form, the mass-entertainment music of the thirties and forties; the same source, with many mixtures, eventually spawned rock and roll, which has become the world music of youth. Fairy tales and folktales have come out of local conditions and over the centuries have entered the mainstream of reading.

In Canada, as elsewhere, up to and even beyond the Second World War, strong regional cultures existed, and they provided a good deal of entertainment that was original, locally oriented, yet universal in themes and values; in addition, such culture was connected historically to older traditions. Religious themes, themes of work, farming, or sailing, individual and social tragedies, and themes of the supernatural linked this material not only to the real lives and beliefs of the people who produced it but also to their own diverse pasts. And the handing down of themes and values (and in some cases of the artworks themselves) created a sense of connection with place and the past, a sense of rooting and continuity that made for a healthy and rich community.[5]

The negative aspects of this regionalism – narrowness, intolerance – were somewhat compensated for by the sense of innate meaningfulness provided for each individual in such communities, and though a lack of artistic complexity might sometimes be evident in the products of these rooted cultures, there were built-in safeguards against vulgarity, cheapness of effect, and the calculated degrading of the audience, which we see as one of the major aspects of contemporary mass culture.

In old Catholic Quebec, in the Maritimes, among Anglo-Canadians in Ontario, among the Ukrainians or Doukhobors on the Prairies, strong traditions endured and in many cases fed the emerging mass culture. Music, radio plays, and films in the popular vein drew upon these sources, just as the aesthetic or serious culture turned to them to create poetry, plays, novels, music, and painting that expressed something of the intrinsic experience of being a Canadian.

That these traditions at first overshadowed the cultures of Native Canadians is a historical tragedy, but every one of these individual cultures, or subcultures, was to go through a process of erosion, transformation, and assimilation, resulting in a kind of "mummification" in relation to the reigning mass culture. These folk-rooted subcultures, when they didn't disappear, lost vitality and began to enshrine nostalgic memories, becoming "grandmother's world" rather than living realities. Their values would be recovered only through often spurious commercial promotions (the theme park idea), or would reappear in the work of serious contemporary artists seeking authentic roots and attempting to escape from the superficial and soulless "masscult" promoted by the media.

Understandably proponents of Canadian popular or entertainment culture – Canadian radio and television shows, films, popular books – estimate "Canadian content" by means of widely varying criteria (though few of them are as bizarre as those chosen by the CRTC). Yet one thing that surely guarantees the Canadianness of these (occasionally successful, often mediocre) products is a link to genuine folk or traditional sources, to a recognizable Canadian landscape, or to a local subculture. Quebec popular culture through the twenties, thirties and forties is replete with examples; some of the early CBC Radio shows display this connection; the Nelvana comic, with its reputed link to Inuit stories, may be a dubious example – nonetheless, the idea of the magic North appears there; the CBC television series *The Newcomers* reflected the lives of Canada's founding groups and their several environments with considerable skill; *The Beachcombers,* though tepid as drama, used the B.C. landscape, while *Seeing Things* occasionally flashed some sense of the Italian subculture in Toronto. *Don Messer's Jubilee,* appalling to many, had a genuine Maritime hominess. And one might argue that in these terms *Nanook of the North,* the famous documentary by the Irishman Robert Flaherty, is more authentically Canadian than shows bankrolled, written, and shot in Toronto or Vancouver (*The X-Files,* for example), which pretend that the setting is Indianapolis or Cleveland. (I have already quoted Peter Harcourt's observation about the place-and-family orientation of most Canadian films.) It is interesting, too, from the point of view of regional anchoring, that while Canadian hockey broadcasters almost always identify the local origins (which are still mostly Canadian) of the players, the American networks, covering the same games, never mention the players' Canadian birthplaces. That a winger or a goalie comes from Papineauville or St. Catharines (even if we hear about it via Don Cherry's outrageous chauvinism) is increasingly important to Canadians as they struggle to retain the sense of hockey as the national sport and not merely as some entertainment adjunct of the Disney Corporation.

The Americanization of the entertainment culture has gone far, and will go much farther in the next century. The arrival of the supermedia, of the new and converging technologies, will make it impossible for the old-fashioned protectionism to function. If the ban on comics of 1941-46 existed today, it would easily be circumvented by electronic means. There is no longer any possibility of closing our borders to the world. Because of this, and because of the inroads already made on the Canadian psyche by American products, government schemes to promote Canadian popular entertainment over foreign material seem rather futile. Canada has produced one superstar after another, yet we have no "entertainment industry," and there is no prospect of ever having one. It is perhaps unreasonable to expect that we should have one, in view of our population and our vulnerability to the American giant next door. The idea of the national government expending vast sums of money to give Canadians what they *don't* want was never a sensible one, and it has even less appeal in an era of tight money. And one reason why many Canadians don't want entertainment blatantly labelled "Canadian" is because they suspect its authenticity. By contrast the American stuff seems to be "natural," just for fun, without ideological trappings. This, of course, is nonsense, but it is one of the great strengths of American entertainment culture that it can successfully mask its ideology as "pure entertainment." (It cons others by first sincerely conning itself.) I will address some aspects of this issue shortly. Here it must be noted that even in view of the complications just cited, the CRTC's Canadian-content rules seem minimal, and though they are unwieldy and often irrational, in the absence of some other vigorous gesture in favour of Canadian cultural sovereignty it would be foolish not to try to rationalize and strengthen them.

Legislation, however, must retain contact with reality. Are Canadians so off the mark in being suspicious of attempts to force Canadian content on them when the terms of such content are so ambiguous? In my view, entertainment culture everywhere is so bound up with capitalistic principles of profit and loss, supply and demand, that it would be absurd to assume that we could somehow harness such material to a national purpose. Canadian popular entertainers who "make it" (and a great many do) need no support from government, and in most cases deserve none, because in the act of making it, they have shed most of what might constitute the uniqueness of their Canadian perspective.[6] There are some entertainers of whom this is clearly not true, and who occupy the boundary land between cultural levels, a Leonard Cohen, a Gordon Lightfoot, a Gilles Vigneault. This kind of artist clearly has a strong claim to be treated as a potent Canadian (or Québécois) cultural force, but this is clearly not true for music stars such as Bryan Adams or k. d. lang. Enterprising Canadian producers will go on exploiting the international markets, but this will not be a cultural triumph, chiefly a financial one: their work will not express very much of Canada. Harlequin Books is a notable and, to many, a painful example. We should certainly celebrate the achievements of our popular entertainers, just as we should applaud the foresight and finesse of such media entrepreneurs as Moses Znaimer and Michael MacMillan, the little-known but enterprising chairman of Atlantis Films. We can be grateful for whatever positive results such success stories create for Canada, but it is a mistake, I think, to lump these kinds of achievements together with those of our aesthetic culture. We are talking about entertainment here, and entertainment, if it is successful, pays. That Canadian entertainers, such as William Shatner, not only get rich but also, in so doing, become powerful representatives of American ideologies only adds a dimension of irony to the situation, but the irony has been repeated many times.

The real answer to the dominance of American entertainment culture is twofold. First, Canada must strengthen and protect its aesthetic culture, for such culture provides the depth of perspective, the critical material, and the emotional anchoring that make resistance to the super-ficialities of international pop culture a certainty. We need to answer schlock and middlebrow pabulum, not with our own homemade schlock and middlebrow pabulum, but with responses of quality. We need *Finlandia* (or better still, *Four Legends,* or Symphony No. 4). We need *War and Peace,* Fellini's *I Vitelloni* or *La Strada,* and the equivalent of Verdi's "Va, pensiero" – not Canadian versions of *Married with Children* or *Seinfeld*; and thanks to several decades of serious cultural activity, we *are* getting works of high quality.[7]

Second, we need to be more critically aware of the power of the arts, of the new media, and of their interactions. These are areas in which, despite many pleas for change, our educational system has failed us. In the country of Harold Innis, of McLuhan and Gould, this failure is par-ticularly painful (see chapter 9). For a start we might try to understand the power of the popular media to carry cultural messages, the power of critique and depth perception generated by serious culture, and the his-torical situation that has led us into a postmodern era in which many of the old boundaries between levels of culture are fast dissolving.

American analysts of popular culture alert us to the latent content of much of what passes for "pure entertainment," material that has been devoured for decades by Canadian audiences who have been beguiled by the artful packaging, by the "sincerity" of the communication. Richard Slotkin, in two lengthy studies, has demonstrated the pervasive presence of the frontier myth in American culture, uncovering its barely concealed imagery of conflict and conquest, its focus on the violently driven "six-gun" hero. He has noted the ubiquity of this key story and others like it (all seemingly innocent of any message), and has shown how such stories reflect, support, and sometimes assuage the guilt of American political actions that, without the trappings of pseudo-heroism, would seem merely brutal.[8]

Slotkin's analysis makes clear that an especially potent source of mythological material lies in popular literature, where stereotypes reign and the often complex strategies of high art yield to more sim-plified presentations. In this context "pure entertainment" becomes capable of embodying a whole range of unexamined national assump-tions and of presenting them with compelling force under the guise of entertainment.

A powerful example of this process emerges in another analysis, *The American Monomyth,* by John Shelton Lawrence and Robert Jewett. These writers track American popular literature through several decades (from about 1900 to 1950); in the process they uncover a focal story, which tells of the innocent settlement threatened (always by external forces) and rescued by the superhero, an idealistic loner whose resort to violence is excused by his sexual purity. This "divinely cool" redeemer restores the settlement and disappears; Eden is maintained without the necessity of confronting the Fall (arguably the most profound aspect of the Eden story), and the evil that should be confronted in the self is invariably projected onto outsiders.[9] Interestingly this analysis confirms the well-known theological critique of American culture by Reinhold Niebuhr, who uncovered the chief irony of American history in the failure of Americans to acknowledge the possibility of evil arising from their presumption of innocence.[10]

The authors convincingly demonstrate the pervasiveness and adaptability of this theme of rescued Eden through what they call the "axial decade" of myth formation in the United States, from about 1929 to the Second World War. Examining texts such as Owen Wister's *The Virginian,* the Buck Rogers stories, the Lone Ranger, Superman, The Shadow, Doc Savage, Heidi, *Jaws,* and *Star Trek,* they show its survival virtually to the present day.[11]

These demonstrations of the potency of popular literature may seem odd in our time, when the perspective on such literature has changed; in fact, we have passed from a long period of naive storytelling (the formation of the popular myths) into a second phase of popular-culture creation. In this phase the original stories, images, and stereotypes are assumed to be well established and familiar to a wide audience; this assumption allows them to be treated ironically, played with, extended, and even related to serious culture. If we compare the original Superman comic strip to the movie remakes, the classic private eye movies to *Chinatown,* the earlier westerns to Clint Eastwood's *Unforgiven,* or the traditional Coca-Cola ads with Andy Warhol's paintings, we can see how both "camp" and a postmodern "playing with culture" emerge from the matrix of a relatively "innocent" popular art. This more sophisticated stage of popular culture might lead some to discount the power of the myths embodied in the original material. "Even Americans don't take those things seriously anymore," it might be said. "Just look how *Star Trek* has evolved!" And some shifts of emphasis are evident – in keeping with social and political changes.

Yet American popular entertainment remains obsessed with American themes and values, and the implication of this obsession for foreign cultures in general, and for Canadian culture in particular, is enormous. Given that Canadians – even more so than other audiences around the world – have been drawn over many decades into associating with this material as if it were their own (though it is hardly the story of Canadian culture), disengagement seems nearly impossible. Canadian psychic space, thanks to the myth-making power of the American entertainment industry, can now be seen as "occupied territory." The sometimes acerbic Yankee baiting among Canadian intellectuals takes place partially because so many of them have woken up to an awareness of their colonized mentalities, and of course have resented it. And some key Canadian texts, those marking the passage to national intellectual and imaginative self-awareness (such as Atwood's *Survival*), have made a point of trying to free Canadians from the particular mix of megalomania, violence, and innocence that so curiously underlies and afflicts American culture and politics.

Although some Canadians seem increasingly unaware of the fact, Canadian culture is fundamentally different than American culture. This is not because of our connection with "the North," as suggested by many. It has little to do with the Canadian mosaic, nor is it a result of our division into the two cultures of anglo and francophone Canada. A more comprehensive view suggests that we have the distinction (if it is a distinction) of being the first postmodern society: multiethnic, introverted, nonaggressive, and cooperative – a society with connections everywhere and fixed boundaries nowhere, one more interested in communication than in self-assertion and conquest.[12]

While this may be partially true, it also misses the mark somewhat. To understand the essence of Canadian society, paradoxically, we might go all the way back to develop a master term introduced by the Romantic poet, John Keats; namely, "negative capability," which Keats defines as the capability "of being in doubts, without any irritable reaching after fact and reason." Keats saw this as the mark of the greatest writers, of Shakespeare in particular.[13] I find the term very suggestive of the Canadian experience and character. We are a country that is condemned to live creatively amid unresolvable tensions. The North is an overwhelming fact, yet we huddle close to the American border, our cities strung across the continent, with the North always at our backs, so to speak. The idea that we will spread out and develop that vast polar hinterland is absurd, yet we continue to assume this as our destiny. As a country, we are trapped in the Siamese-twin image of the two founding nations, doomed to exist as cultures never able to resolve their differences, yet not quite able to part. (I predict that if Quebec separation comes, it will be nothing like a real separation, nothing like the Czech/Slovak split, for example, but simply a further, and more maddening, complexity of "dissonant partnership.")

The various regions of our country, the Maritimes or the West, for example, seem resentful of always being ignored or taken for granted. They claim to hunger after special recognition, or to want greater independence or attention. I suspect that what they really long for is a settled identity and that they dream about some distinctive psychosocial stasis within Canada. But their dreams of harmony are futile because the cardinal principle of being Canadian is "living in tension." The same idea may be applied to our national conceptions of government and social justice. As Canadians, we are decentralized federalists and social-welfare capitalists; we demand both independence and protection; we value our traditions, yet seem almost embarrassed by them; we tolerate our Native people and immigrants, yet often unwittingly bind them to us in ways that frustrate them. We are in every respect the opposite of a monomaniac nation like the United States which, for all its internal diversity and its social and regional conflicts, bubbles with confidence and freezes in a salute full of solemn and reverential awe at the very notion of "America." Canada is condemned to bear its irresolute, tolerant, indomitable, and uncertain soul into the 21st century. Our artists have taught us and will continue to teach us much about the possibility of living in doubt. They will continue to celebrate, not our potential unity, but our permanent place at the tension point of irreconcilable opposites. Only when they abandon this vision, when they try to force the issues, to thrust on us some dogma or superficial resolution, do our artists (not to mention our politicians) violate the spirit of Canada.

This is precisely why I emphasize that if we are to ensure the predominance of Canadian values and the continuing elaboration of truly relevant themes over the next few decades of our history, our national policies must centre on promoting Canadian aesthetic or high culture against popular or mass culture. The American industry has already virtually co-opted the field of popular entertainment, and in view of its ever-tightening control of the new mass media (which will only increase in the next century), this stranglehold shows no signs of being broken. Consider the upsurge in the United States in recent years of the television religious networks and the radio talk shows. Such "innocent" entertainments represent mostly right-wing – and in some cases near-fascist – outpourings, whether they wallow in Jesus ecstasy or writhe in antiliberal, antigovernment hatred and resentment of the G. Gordon Liddy style. Canadian imitators – and they appear every day – inevitably carry some of this political baggage when they jump into such broadcasting.

Because of the "imitation" factor, I disagree with those who advocate the promotion of Canadian arts and culture that are only "Canadian" by virtue of the birthplaces or home bases of the creators. Pop material that is American in theme and manner, that is indistinguishable from the masscult produced by the U.S. entertainment industry, that fails to touch Canadian roots – this is foreign matter, whatever the passport held by its perpetrators. Aesthetic culture that is produced by Canadians, whatever the influences, will almost always have a historical and critical dimension that will rescue it from repeating foreign stereotypes – for that is precisely what serious culture is all about. And if it is argued that a Canadian opera singer performing the work of an American composer, or a Canadian dancer performing the Aaron Copland-Martha Graham *Billy the Kid,* is hardly any different from Bryan Adams doing a rock number conceived in the American manner, I would say: not quite the same. Serious works of art almost always have a perspective that stirs complex thoughts and emotions in the spectator; they are seldom unidimensional.

In arguing for Canadian serious art, I am not in the least suggesting a cultural chauvinism; in art international exchange is often the breath of life. I am merely arguing that we should acknowledge the enormous importance of our serious artists, who – all things being equal – will be in touch with Canadian traditions in a way that is denied to those who must operate within the terms of the American capitalistic system and its mythologies of pseudo-innocence and domination.

Yet the objection may still be made by those familiar with the evolution of aesthetic culture during the last few decades that here, too, integrity is in question, that in many cases what were strong local and national attachments have been undermined by big money allied with new developments in communications, and that the resulting superficial internationalism has led us toward a situation in which there is little to choose from between the pop superstar and the so-called serious artist.

An obvious example is the takeover of the publishing industry by megacorporations, a situation that (some argue) has made the accountant, not the editor, king of the trade, and has undermined the commitment to experiment and to publish works of promise that lack the potential to become instant hits. Or consider classical music, where a conductor such as Herbert von Karajan became a financial potentate and promoter (mostly of his own talents), overextending himself with imperial self-confidence and arrogance. In the wake of his and other such examples, the superstars of classical music, having climbed to the top by means of contests as elaborate if not as absurd as those that used to promote "beauty queens," and with no allegiance to any particular country or region, flit about the world, appear at festivals in Asia one week and in Europe the next, do television shows, and record the same standard repertory again and again.

High culture, too, has largely lost its roots, and has fallen victim to promotional methods that once upon a time would have been resisted even by companies selling cornflakes or beer. A new cynicism has arisen among highbrow music lovers (art lovers have always been cynical, and many highbrow readers don't notice the changes in the book industry until they take up writing themselves). Consumers of aesthetic culture have every reason to share the disillusionment of sports fans, who have lost enormous sympathy for their heroes of diamond or rink after seeing them go on strike to improve salaries that would run many small cities for months on end.

In the light of these changes, the public's traditional anti-intellectualism, its tendency to sneer at contemporary art and to suspect its sincerity, has been given a new impetus. In this postmodern era, when conflicting and mutually incomprehensible styles and artistic aims jostle with one another, when the boundaries of art and nonart often seem tenuous, the gap between popular taste and serious taste is widening. Those interested in aesthetic culture find their interest rarely supported or encouraged by society at large. Despite the high bankrolling of the most successful aesthetic culture, despite its new glitz, despite its mimicking of pop culture's speeded-up rootlessness, it occupies almost no place in the consciousness of the average citizen in North America. News reports, which occasionally deal with science, almost never mention classical music, ballet, or theatre. Book companies go under, galleries close, conductors change places, but with the exception of a few newspapers, these events are seldom taken as significant news by the print media, and television reporting almost completely ignores them.[14]

Perhaps the most visible effect of aesthetic culture's new chic is its increased vulnerability to ridicule by those who fail to understand why certain abstract paintings or "obscene photographs" should be bought and exhibited by public institutions, why taxes should be used to cover the deficits of ballet companies and symphony orchestras, why young poets should be funded by government to write incomprehensible books that almost no one will ever read. In the days when the public's characteristic image of an artist was that of the starving bohemian, a certain public sympathy could be counted on. But when artists seem to be doing well, when brief (and misleading) glimpses afforded by the press suggest that they form a new monied elite, resentments multiply, especially when the works produced are regarded as morally questionable, noncommunicative, or in the nature of a put-on.

Despite the new corruptions that have crept into the marketing and distribution of aesthetic culture (they are perhaps inescapable in a capitalistic society), idealism still thrives among those involved in its creation. The chic, the sly, the self-aggrandizing elements remain, but there are also hosts of veteran theatre people, aspiring and dogged writers, actors, and singers (young and old), as well as musicians, editors of small presses and literary magazines, and filmmakers – these people form in Canada as strong an arts infrastructure as exists anywhere. What is really needed is to ensure that the great reservoir of energy and idealism that exists in such circles is not wasted. Despite the suspicions of many, I would argue that given Canada's position vis-à-vis American entertainment culture, only a comprehensive national plan to strengthen and develop its aesthetic culture (which means connection, or reconnection, with the largest possible, best informed, and most involved audiences) will maintain our national integrity into the next century.

In fact, serious art in its regional, local, and national manifestations is our best hope of continuing to develop a country and a people that can claim independence of mind, a perspective on their own lives, and a sense of the uniqueness of their history. Aesthetic culture, because it encourages depth, reflection, and insight, leads away from the noisy, superficial, transitory, and highly Americanized world of pop culture. If we do not have some avenues to help us escape from and confound the collective, mindless entertainment circus of the mass media, we will be swallowed up; our geographical boundaries may remain intact, but there will be nothing substantial left of the spirit of Canada.

5 The Arts, the New Politics, and the Next Canada

*The emphasis on tribalism, tokenism and toeing the political line
is, if anything, more painful in the realm of culture, which traditionally represents the highest aspirations of the individual, than it
is in other realms of the life of the mind.*
                    – William A. Henry III, *In Defence of Elitism*

B Y THE MID-EIGHTIES Canadians had begun to realize that the
country they knew and had taken for granted was going through
fundamental, and not altogether welcome, changes. Our particular social mix, our balance of rural and urban components, of linguistic
and regional interests, suddenly seemed to be upset. Our relationship to
the natural environment no longer appeared quite so rational and comfortable; our endless resources were seen to be limited; demographics
were changing; the "permanent" treaties concluded with our Native
peoples were being questioned. The old prosperity gave way to a new
financial uncertainty, and economic constraints began to make spending
on the arts look like a dispensable luxury.

During these years, Canada – along with other Western democracies –
saw the left veering away from traditional liberal ideas about the arts and
culture and taking up a position much closer to that of the Marxist bureaucracies, which had demanded for decades conformity to the opportunism
of the Soviet party line. This severing of ties with the older liberal tradition, though surprising, can be seen to have many origins. The contradiction between the high culture of Germany and the degenerate Hitlerian
politics undermined faith in the moral efficacy of the traditional culture.
The Marxist reduction of spiritual values to questions of class interests,
together with successive waves of scientism (each attempting to reestablish
materialistic values on the ruins of the preceding oversimplifications),
played a part. The critical assault on religious faith and idealistic philosophy

alike helped to devalue traditional ideas of the transcendent and to shift the emphasis to the "hard" realities of class and economics. Free will and the human power of inwardness, the originating power of the imagination, were denied. Thus, ideas of art and culture that might have seemed more appropriate in the Stalinist Soviet Union arose to displace traditional Western values, and the notion that art was first of all an ideological instrument became widely held, especially in academic circles.[1]

The increasing politicization of arts and cultural issues, in both Canada and the United States, encompassed the mobilization of black power, the arrival of the new feminism, the struggle for gay rights, a well-organized activism on the part of minorities of all kinds, and a new outspokenness on the part of the culturally disenfranchised – all of which challenged the assumptions of the majority and the old elites.

The ancient idea that the arts and culture in their ultimate reaches transcend the everyday life of the tribe, that they lead to eternal truths, or to a universally valid human wisdom, was cast aside. Culture was no longer a sphere of objective contemplation, a treasure house of the best and most profound of human thoughts and values, an instrument for the discovery of psychological and moral truth. Culture, far from being (as Matthew Arnold suggested) the opposite of anarchy, was very often a synonym for oppression, the instrument of domination of a social class, the preserve of the powerful few, whose idealisms were merely a cover for political and social control. The older notion of culture, inherited from Greece and the Middle Ages, secularized and transmitted to the 20th century through liberal thought, and universally accepted as part of the spiritual charter of our democratic society, was challenged by revisionist politics.[2]

History itself must be rewritten, said the revisionists, art must express the struggles of the oppressed for social and political equality, the status quo must be challenged, but – and this is the important point – this was not merely a call for minorities to enter the democratic sphere of culture (they had been doing that for generations). It was a change of the rules, a new charter suggesting that because the main traditions of Western society constituted a thinly veiled conspiracy against those who did not hold power, radical means of subversion of the power of the reigning culture and values were quite in order.

Within a remarkably short time, Canadian cultural life was transformed: fresh talents emerged out of the new diversity. Benefits were apparent: some of the art that resulted reflected the new Canada in a powerful way, and aesthetic culture was enriched. Here we seemed to have proof, if proof were needed, that energetic minorities with a powerful vision of their own lived realities, previously unreported or suppressed, could challenge, and by challenging overcome, at least part of the unconsciousness and stupidity of a complacent majority.

Yet for some of these previously disenfranchised groups, for some individuals, this was hardly enough. They were not content to become parts of a new Canadian mosaic; their mission would only be accomplished when the older parts of the mosaic crumbled. Some set themselves up as censors; others opportunistically accepted their access to power and used it to condemn the system. We had seen this phenomenon before – this resentment, this love of faction, this bitter intransigence – in the Leninist-Trotskyite battles of the thirties; among the leftist groups that were in constant enmity during the Spanish Civil War; among the outlawed revolutionary cadres in Africa and South America, factions that often hated each other much more than they hated the reigning governments.

In all this, multiculturalism threatened to become "multifactionism" and to challenge even Canada's capacity to incorporate and hold together seemingly irreconcilable opposites. Intransigence, a fear of being "co-opted" that amounted to paranoia, fanaticism of a dour and unbending kind, and an ideological rancour against "male, white, Western, monied culture" possessed many individuals and gradually sapped the exhilaration of the cultural nationalism of the sixties and seventies. ("Fanaticism consists in redoubling your effort when you have forgotten your aim," George Santayana once wrote.)

The response of the so-called cultural establishment to this new wave of fanaticism was (at first) timid, uncertain, and often accommodating – *gutless* would probably be the most accurate word. Small *l* liberalism, with its generosity of view, its tolerance, its sense of intellectual fair play, and its love of freedom of expression found itself quite unable to cope. Artists and professors, writers and broadcasters, curators and museum directors outdid themselves to escape the dreaded possibility that they might offend some vocal minority. What matter how unreasonable the protest or complaint? To be charged with racial or ethnic bias, or with sexism, was like being accused of child molesting: you were guilty until you could prove yourself innocent. A new "treason of the clerks," a betrayal of culture by the intellectuals, was in progress. And where the left actually held power (as in the case of Bob Rae's government in Ontario), a new class of *apparatchiki* emerged and gleefully began to apply their social quotas to the creative process.

As always, creativity paid a severe price as a result of the politicization of the arts. Racial, ethnic, and gender criteria, overt or assumed, began to determine more and more which art and artists would be supported or publicized. Art and culture that proved unacceptable to minorities, or to special-interest groups, stood little chance of getting serious exposure, or of surviving any well-organized campaign of political disruption. Freedom of expression was threatened by new shibboleths and taboos, which attempted to suppress those aspects of traditional discourse deemed – sometimes on very slender grounds – to be racist, sexist, or otherwise offensive to a particular social group. Both on the national and the regional level, agencies began to endorse policies that supported the notion that the chief value of art is to promote social harmony. Dangerous and often ill-conceived terms and concepts such as "political correctness," "appropriation of voice," and "cultural diversity" threatened fundamental notions of excellence, not to mention the traditional conception of the artist's freedom of imagination. (And all of this served the careers of quite a few cultural climbers, who exploited the confusion and increasingly uneasy goodwill of the traditionalists and the arts establishment to serve their own purposes.)

Clearly it was not the aspirations of the cultural have-nots that were disturbing to many fair-minded observers. Nor was it this latest exposure of the contradictions between traditional notions of high culture and the social corruptions of capitalism: generations of liberal critics had made these contradictions clear. It was the sense that criteria of excellence were being undermined in the name of a spurious equality, that in the emerging technopoly of the left, the letter would ultimately kill the spirit, freedom would be sacrificed in the name of the shibboleth of equality, while art would be denied the power to reflect reality, rather than someone's ideological fix on it.

In all of this, in Canada, the unfolding of a national purpose in the arts and culture, the sense of self-definition and synthesis implicit in the sixties and seventies, seemed to falter; enrichment and updating (or *perestroika*) were one thing; factions and fear mongering were something else.

The Canada Council, despite its insistence on its traditional "arm's-length" distance from government (interpreted to mean that artists should be funded on the basis of merit only), was especially vulnerable to the stresses of the new political climate (see also chapter 6). "Cultural diversity" (the chosen euphemism for the policy of providing special opportunities for minorities and ethnic and racial groups) was first embraced in 1989 and pursued systematically for the next several years by means of a series of new appointments, administrative changes, conferences, policy statements, and the like.[3] An Advisory Committee for Racial Equality in the Arts (a very strange concept when you think about it) was created in 1990, along with the First People's Advisory Committee on the Arts. An equity coordinator was hired; Canada Council documents were scanned for "ethnocentric bias"; the very term "professionalism" was redefined, presumably to accommodate those deserving minorities who couldn't or wouldn't meet the old standards. At the same time, juries were provided with representatives of minority groups, and the practice of using "special assessors" for non-Western art forms was increased.

This record indicates that the Council, in the familiar manner of a semiofficial government organization vulnerable to the criticism of zealous minorities, was mightily concerned to be as proactive as possible on behalf of ethnic artists. Yet one of the cornerstones of Council policy, that artistic quality alone should decide who gets the grants, was clearly incompatible with such politically motivated rule making. It was assumed that if you wish to redress the injustices minorities have suffered, you cannot hold strictly to the merit principle; you may also have to change institutional ground rules in order to accommodate cultural differences. The Council had begun to change these rules, yet paid lip service to the traditional policies and inevitably got caught.

In 1992 Joyce Zemans, a very able Council director, was reported by Stephen Godfrey in the *Globe and Mail* as articulating a new Council policy on appropriation of voice (namely, don't try it if you want a Council grant).[4] The ensuing furor had a few bright notes, among them letters from Timothy Findley, Neil Bissoondath, and Alberto Manguel (also in the *Globe and Mail*) defending the old idea of artistic freedom.[5] Zemans's damage-control strategy was to deny that there had been a change of policy and to suggest that the Council had attempted to legislate equity of opportunity, not to interfere with artistic freedom.[6] When confronted by the backlash of the established arts community (and when pressed by Peter Gzowski in an interview), she backed away completely from the notion of appropriation of voice.

Despite this uproar the Council's criteria for funding were redefined in 1993 to "ensure that all qualifying organizations of all cultures will have access to Council on an equal basis."[7] (The word *qualifying* begins to look weak in the context.) A separate "Aboriginal Unit" within the Council was even considered, suggesting that fairness was a matter of being judged by one's own ethnic peers.[8] Curiously the term "classical music" was decreed to refer no longer to the Western tradition.[9]

Meanwhile publishers (and even the large ones still hungered for government grants) fell over themselves to conform to what they imagined to be the official (though unacknowledged) politics. In 1993 it was decided by some members of the editorial board at one well-known Toronto small press that only "books by women" were acceptable to complete that year's list.[10] Quality, the board members assured themselves, was what they wanted – but quality would only count if the writer were a woman. The same firm was offered an engaging short novel describing the life of an Ecuadorian woman who eventually moves to Montreal. The young author (a white male Canadian), a Spanish speaker closely familiar with his subject, had already published well-received fiction in somewhat the same vein. In private the small press's publisher admitted that, due to what he perceived as the prevailing politics of the major government grant organizations, it would be better if the young white male author were an Ecuadorian woman. Later, an outside academic reader also raised concerns about voice appropriation in the novel under consideration. Needless to say, the small press didn't publish the book.[11]

The culminating point of this alarming retreat from the principle of objectivity, and the most blatant nose thumbing at the supposed "white establishment," was perhaps the "Writing Thru Race" conference, held in Vancouver from June 20 to July 3, 1994, and attended by 180 people.[12] This event, which banned white writers from the afternoon workshops, was funded by the City of Vancouver and the British Columbia Ministry of Tourism ($9,500), by private contributions from artists and writers, and by the Canada Council ($10,000).[13] Former federal heritage minister Michel Dupuy, responding to Reform Party criticism of the conference as racist, refused to release federal funding – for which he was criticized by the Writers' Union (though a considerable number of members disapproved of the form of the conference).[14]

Roy Miki, a West Coast writer and chair of the Racial Minorities Committee of the Writers' Union, suggested that this "conference of First Nations Writers and Writers of Colour" had been "premised on the belief that the Writers' Union was not sensitive to First Nations Writers."[15] Sensitivity of the wrong kind was certainly in evidence, however, at the Writers' Union meetings in which this issue was debated. Rationality, good manners, and communications skills degenerated; name calling, obscenity, and hysteria – according to several nonmembers in attendance – ruled the day.[16] The deliberations of the Vancouver conference itself were small encouragement to at least some writers of colour, who sought encouragement for their writing and found themselves shouldered toward a politics of confrontation for which they had little taste. The success of the event was in the sphere of publicity; the banning of whites was the chief aspect covered, by both domestic and foreign press.[17]

The official support given to the conference, however, raised some serious issues. Had the funding been completely private, they would not have come up, though the event would have been equally distasteful. Why should taxpayers pay for a racist conference? If blacks had been banned from meetings of an all-white literary conference, the uproar would have been monumental. The "writers of pallour" who supported this political gambit seemed to fit Neil Bissoondath's description of "guilt-ridden white liberals [who] feel they are expiating the political sins of their fathers."[18]

A few months later, Bissoondath himself became the subject of a storm that centred on the related, but even broader, issue of multiculturalism. *Selling Illusions: The Cult of Multiculturalism in Canada* stirred up a lively debate on the subject, some of which was on a high level, though a few self-appointed ethnic spokespersons stooped to racial slurs. Bissoondath's strongest point, however, was touched on by several commentators and comes down to this: if our society fractures into competing interest groups, each of which refuses to acculturate to Canada, to integrate and adapt to a new style of life, a new kind of existence here, then there is little hope of our national survival.[19] Thus, while Sheila Finestone, secretary of state for multiculturalism, responded to Bissoondath by suggesting that "Canada has no national culture," Michael Valpy argued convincingly in a *Globe and Mail* article that "if the choice is unfettered, there will be too little left at the core to call Canadian values, Canadian norms, Canadian ethics, Canadian mythologies, Canadian culture, a Canadian way of life."[20]

We might take to heart (and apply to Canada) the words of William A. Henry III, an American writer confronting a similar fracturing of society, a similar attack on mainstream values by politically obsessed minorities:

> The past that made our culture is a seamless web. The attitudes one may
> lament in the present are inextricable from the attitudes that spawned a
> desirable modern world. And the past need not be ashamed of itself, nor
> we for it, that it included racism and sexism and homophobia and other
> offences against modern notions of human rights. Human beings are an
> evolving species, morally as well as biologically. To get to where we are
> we had to come from somewhere less humane. An imperfect world is not
> the same thing as a worthless one.[21]

No doubt these words would raise the ire and wound the tender souls of many Anglo-Canadian intellectuals, who still spend far too much time apologizing for their own traditions, who waste energy in bemoaning the supposed vice of "Eurocentrism," a perspective that (we are told) assumes too blithely that the great Western tradition of art and culture is the only one worth taking seriously.[22] This current intellectual breast beating is a long-delayed and hugely exaggerated compensation for the arrogance of certain 19th-century writers, such as Lord Macaulay and Alfred Tennyson, who dismissed Eastern cultures in particular as insignificant. (Other world cultures were regarded as merely "primitive."[23] A correction was needed to counteract such arrogance (and ignorance), but we are now approaching absurdity. The tradition of Plato, Dante, Michelangelo, Bach, Goethe, Wagner, Tolstoy, Cézanne – the great Greek-Hebraic-Christian-Enlightenment-Romantic-Modern Western tradition – *is* arguably (I repeat, *arguably*) superior to all others, which is not to denigrate the magnificent traditions of China or the Indian sub-continent, its only real world rivals.

No fair-minded person could doubt that any future planetary culture would gain infinite riches from the non-Western traditions, but that is no reason to apologize for our own heritage, or to assume that its centrality is mainly a result of imperialism and gunboat diplomacy. Those who come to Western countries such as Canada should be prepared to accept and acknowledge our great traditions, and should not expect to maintain their own without regard to the culture that surrounds them, acting as if they had never emigrated. If I were to go to China or India or Arabia or central Africa or the Caribbean and settle down, I hope I would be sensible and humble enough to accept the richness of the cultures I find there, and not to insist that schools teach my traditions, that my children be given special access and representation, so that my culture can have a voice. I would hope to maintain a private and familial contact with my past, but would not insist that public cultural policies be turned upside down to placate me.

As for accommodating our own minorities, it goes without saying that Canadian artists and cultural officials get little credit from minorities for their "sensitive revisions" of the past. This should have been amply clear after the unfortunate *Into the Heart of Africa* exhibition that opened at the Royal Ontario Museum (ROM) in November 1989 and closed a year later after an almost unprecedented outcry and continuous picketing by black groups. The curator, Jeanne Cannizzo, had to resign from her teaching position at the University of Toronto following months of harassment by students and by members of a protest group calling itself the Coalition for the Truth About Africa – academic freedom has suffered greatly under the pressures of the new politics.[24]

The subject of the ROM exhibition was (chiefly) the Canadian missionary presence in turn-of-the-century Africa. The exhibition was designed to allow the viewer freely to enter this world, and the assumption was that the artifacts, images, and writings displayed would, in effect, do the job of self-exposure. Suitable posted warnings should have cued the public that outrageously colonialist and racist attitudes were being shown in order to provide historical perspective on a sad chapter of Western history.[25] But irony is seldom understood by those with deep wounds or narrow agendas. The pressure brought upon the museum is perhaps understandable, but nonetheless unacceptable. Addressing the Museum Trustee Association two years later, Allan Gotlieb, then chair of the Canada Council, made the following general (and surely admirable) statement: "In a democratic society, the views of all citizens must be respected, but in the name of the commonweal of the artistic community and society itself, we must resist attempts by political interests to manipulate artistic institutions for their own purposes."[26]

By 1992, however, curators at our national institutions seemed to have learned how to accommodate the new politics and to do some manipulating of their own. It was the year of the anniversary of the Columbus voyage to the Caribbean, and there was a general fear among institutions and promoters that attempts to "celebrate" this event would arouse the ire of Native groups and result in controversies and boycotts. In an ingenious effort to circumvent this kind of controversy, the Canadian Museum of Civilization offered an exhibition entitled *Indigena*. The curators of the exhibition set the tone by asking a number of Canadian Native artists "to address such issues as discovery, colonization, cultural critique and tenacity . . . and reflect upon the values and ethics of the colonial process on which the Euro-American societies were based."[27] In other words, the Native artists were not only invited but also virtually compelled to turn their art into a propagandistic outburst directed at mainstream society, at Western history, which could only be seen under the circumstances in an evil and oppressive light. But however sorry the record, to attempt to represent history so one-sidedly is inexcusable. Quality control, the possibilities of art as the revelation of truth, as a healing event, these were thrown aside and the artists given rein (naturally at taxpayers' expense) to pillory, assault, and play the political game for all it was worth. One sympathetic, intelligent reviewer of distinctly leftist sympathies wondered whether he was seeing a shared vision of history or whether the artists (and audience) were "dancing to a strong curatorial tune?"[28] He noted that this exhibition "also demands of an audience a good deal of patience, not to say a little masochism," and suggested that it seemed "torn between its desire for strong statement and its identity as a platform for art."[29]

In fact, the exhibition, by the standards of aesthetics, was appalling: angry scrawls and slingshot petulance doing duty for artistic insight, exactness, and technical competence. Far from finding myself engaged, I found that my feelings of anger and sympathy on behalf of the Native cause were temporarily snuffed out, probably the reverse of what the curators had intended. One has to be careful when one tries to manipulate art to serve a cause.

When it comes to censorship and attacks on artistic freedom of expression, we have grown used to the absurdities practised by the entrenched power interests; we take for granted the vehemence of the patriotic and the righteous. An attempt from roughly these quarters to obliterate freedom of expression about historical events was visible (also in 1992) in the protest of Canadian veterans over the CBC/NFB documentary *The Valour and the Horror.* This protest resulted in Senate committee hearings, criticism from the CBC ombudsman and, shamefully, a CBC expression of regret for "any distress" caused, though the series was creative and powerful and not defamatory of veterans.[30]

But with the new politicizing of our artistic and cultural life, it is not chiefly the old sources of censorship and repression we have to deal with; it is self-declared leftists and the proponents of "social justice and progress" who currently offer the greatest threat to artistic freedom During the Bob Rae era in Ontario, this threat became painfully clear when Minister of Culture, Tourism, and Recreation Karen Haslam launched an assault on the Art Gallery of Ontario, which was later shut down for a time.[31] Among her interferences was the creation of a "task force," which was to "ensure that the AGO's access, educational and outreach activities and support for artists in communities throughout the province reflect the diversity of Ontario."[32]

The message of the NDP government (that equality is more important than quality) was further driven home by pressure on universities to make sure that their classrooms would be "comfortable" places for all students. Not only did this threaten the free expression that is integral to academic discourse, but it also offered an open invitation to any number of insecure, unhappy, unsophisticated, or malicious students to complain formally about their instructors' supposed "insensitivity" to gender, race, sexual politics, and the like. Nor was the malaise confined to Ontario. In a notorious case that received wide attention during 1994 and 1995, the University of British Columbia's political science department was accused of systemic racism and other failings. A lengthy investigation followed, conducted by an outsider whose report turned out to be as expensive as it was indecisive and nonspecific (it was condemned by noted jurist Tom Berger and by the B.C. Civil Liberties Association). This report, however, resulted in the suspension of admissions to the political science graduate program and in other desperate and ill-considered measures adopted by the university administration before general outrage, and a large dose of common sense, began to restore some sanity to the situation.[33]

The examples could be multiplied, but I believe the point has been made: the root of such evils lies in the overvaluation of the political dimension in the arts and the often cynical (and sometimes misguidedly idealistic) use of the arts and culture by the left and by minorities to achieve political ends.

Without the infusion of talent, the new perspectives, the economic initiatives, and the telling examples of courage amid adversity provided by new immigrants, this would be an immeasurably poorer country. Nor need ethnic diversity constitute a problem – far from it. Mario Bernardi, Oscar Peterson, Joy Kogawa, William Kurelek, Raymond Moriyama, Michael Ondaatje – the list of contributions to Canada's arts and culture made by Canadians of neither French nor British origins is clearly outstanding. Nonetheless there is a great difference between joining a culture and becoming an advocate for a ghetto politics that seeks to overturn a culture. As Mavor Moore has suggested, as early as 1989, "What price multiculture, if culture fails?"[34] Canada has been evolving into something different from the historical multicultural Anglo-French fact. This evolution will be creatively continued by members of various ethnic groups – but not if they insist on their absolute separateness and victimhood, and not if they are bent on overturning all the traditional values of the main culture.

Both those who advocate some specific subcultural agenda and those who follow the Marxist idea of class warfare are the enemies of art and culture. Although they may disagree with one another on many issues, they agree in attempting to use art chiefly to further ideological purposes.[35]

Certainly there is a political side to art, yet most classical music, abstract painting, and lyric poetry have little political content; if they raise moral or political issues, if they shock and challenge, it is usually only because the audience cannot grasp their forms or structures. Drama of all kinds and especially fiction, however, are often judged on moral grounds, and today they – together with traditional representational art – receive most of the attention of critics determined to introduce race, class, and gender issues into aesthetics.

The current ideologues pretend that you can talk about politics as a way of encompassing art. This is not possible. The Muslims who denounce Salman Rushdie's *The Satanic Verses* because they see the book as an insult to Islam are clearly not talking about art (though they could certainly do so by suggesting, for example, that the book renders Muhammad poorly). Their point of view is unacceptable; because Western intellectuals are skeptical of religion, anyway, they have no trouble seeing this. But to condemn a complex work of art because it derides or opposes the poor, Marxists, homosexuals, or women is to adopt the same attitude as the Muslim condemners of Rushdie (and to follow, ultimately, the ideas of the Catholic Inquisition or the Stalinists), namely, that the reigning ideology is always the issue, even when other issues appear to be on the table. To deal with art largely on the basis of its politics or morality, or in terms of what Nietzsche called *ressentiment* against power structures, is to begin to tear the artwork apart, a dire process rationalized and euphemized under the term "deconstruction."

We are told by Marxist academics that the ideal of art held up by present aesthetic culture is, in fact, a recent one, a product chiefly of 19th-century bourgeois ideals; that its claim to spiritual profundity is undermined by its function in preserving class dominance; and that in any case the "classical ideal" was born amid oligarchy and tyranny, slavery, exploitation, and colonialism. In other words, we are given a version of art and high culture that judges them to be offshoots of a discredited economic and social reality.

In this reading of culture, the artwork, however profound and complex, and the artist, however iconoclastic and original, are understood as secondary phenomena compared to the abiding reality of class oppression, grounded in economics. What's more, the artist and his or her work – in this view – are often deemed guilty by association; they are collaborators in the injustices of an unreformed society. Naturally, from this perspective, the power of individual creativity is denied or diminished, while the claim that art is able to speak of more than material values is treated as a smoke screen.

There are so many things wrong with this view that it is hard to know where to begin to refute it. The ideals of high art have evolved since the far past; the 19th century neither plucked them from thin air nor appropriated them to cover its brutalities. History is process and change; there is no perfect point from which to regard it (except possibly that of eternity), and while fashions and interpretations change, certain principles seem to develop, enriching each generation because creative individuals struggle to embody them anew in art and thought. What is truth? What meaning has life? Are there forces higher than humanity? How can we deal with the lower impulses? What face do we give to good, or to evil? How do we imagine the living world? The human soul?

It is doubtful whether the world will ever banish material injustice or cure social evil; art challenges these problems, not only by exposing them but also by engaging our senses in complex ways so as to lead us beyond both the brutalities of matter and the imprisonment of ideas in abstract theorizings. The nemesis of art is neither collusion with power nor deceitfulness but single-minded righteousness and an insistence on truths of the narrowest kind. The creative unconscious, prodigal and prodigious, cannot follow the formulas of virtue, or wear blinders in the face of chaos. Anarchy, capitalism, and even the milder forms of tyranny may serve the artist well (and art, in turn, does much to mitigate their brutalities), but societies professing devotion to social betterment through the application of rational principles always end up trying to destroy art.

I would suggest that the discussion of aesthetics remains central to art, that the work of art must be perceived sui generis, in terms of its (often flawed) wholeness; it must be judged for the skill and beauty with which it contributes to the dialogue of humanity, and not be torn apart, sanctified merely by its historical context, or praised because it lends support to the critic's political agenda.[36] I define an aesthetic judgement as one that centres on the form and structure of a given work, showing to what extent that work may lead us to an understanding of life's complexity and of the truth of existence. Such a judgement might determine whether the form is an empty shell or merely a facade – a deceptive screen or illusion – that hides the truth from us. I do not believe that good structure can serve to deceive us about the truth-telling capacities of the artwork. When we encounter a work with a complex, intellectually sophisticated, emotionally rich structure; find noble simplicity, compelling energy, or sublimity; or are convinced, through its intrinsic honesty and power, of the work's vision of life, there must be truth.

Art at its greatest suggests an intrinsic order in the universe, a higher reality, a beauty and goodness that take us as close to the infinite as does the wisdom of the greatest spiritual teachers and mystics. True art is intrinsically "anti-evil," because it refuses to simplify life, to override it in the name of slogans, of mechanism, because it refuses to accept superficial categories of morality.

The objection is sometimes raised that the art ideal reveals its inadequacy in the face of a blatantly evil politics. Two questions are often asked. The first has to do with the professed love and appreciation of aesthetic beauty by those committing monstrously evil acts: for example, how can a Nazi love Mozart? The idea seems appalling, yet we know that many Nazis had a profound and no doubt valid appreciation of some of the greatest works of Western art. The second question is related and touches on the essence of the artwork itself. If a Nazi can find beauty in great art, doesn't it prove that the notion that such a work might have an intrinsic power to reveal something honest about life (never mind something eternal or ideal) is illusory?[37] Isn't it clear that art is totally conditioned and shaped by society and history, and so riddled through with the biases and agendas of the "haves" (who mostly pay for it) as to be continually in need of deconstruction? Doesn't the Nazi's sincere love of Mozart or Piero della Francesca demonstrate that art has no power to affect us, other than the power we give it? Doesn't it show that high art has no essential meaning, that the claim that it embodies an ideal, something objective and universal, transcending a given social and political milieu is false?[38]

It shows nothing of the kind. There seems to be no innate necessity for human beings to love the order and beauty revealed by art (and by other aspects of life); it's clear that we have invented plenty of psychological tricks to avoid dealing with the moral imperatives suggested by that beauty and order. We are quite capable of constructing our experiences so as to protect ourselves from the ultimate implications of even the deepest truths. Even though profound art might not carry specifics against evil actions, against hatred or murder, in order to enjoy it, and still do these things, we must shut down part of our minds. The imperviousness of some to the power of moral elevation often present in great art suggests the weakness of human nature; it does not reflect on the power of art to transform us. Human beings have an infinite capacity for "compartmentalization." We probably learn this perverse skill in childhood, playing one parent against the other. Later we find that we have unconsciously modified our personae (the faces we present to the world) to suit any situation. Thus, a male athlete is a self-controlled hero to his teammates, but beats his wife; the contradiction is not felt as such by him. Likewise a Nazi may enjoy the aesthetics of music that speaks of love and beauty while murdering Jews. That Hitler could appreciate the sublime symphonies of Bruckner confirms not the lack of intrinsic beauty in the music but the almost infinite capacity for perversion in human nature.[39] We know from experience that some art has the power to lift us out of our narrow selves and to show us a world of beauty or an inner logic of life that we defy at our peril. To obscure this unique power of art by blatant manifestos and sour prohibitions is to blindfold humanity in order to make it virtuous.

With the focus on aesthetics, the spectre of censorship is kept at bay; we are reminded that there are no forbidden subjects, only inadequate treatments. In a novel, if a character is rendered complexly and his or her evil is not excused, if we are shown the complexity of life and human nature, then there is a huge gain for society, whatever the overt morality espoused by the writer. ("Trust the tale, not the teller," advised D. H. Lawrence.) Why shouldn't a writer manage to write a novel exhibiting a sympathetic fascist hero, or write movingly of Paul Bernardo (the Toronto man convicted of raping, torturing, and murdering two young women)? A novel that makes us feel sympathetic to Bernardo, despite his heinous crimes, would probably be a great novel (because it would have to probe so deeply into human nature, into places where the deep roots of good and evil, free will and compulsion, cruelty and love blur and mingle). Far from banning it, we should make sure it is read as widely as possible. The politics of the writer (or the beholder) is almost the worst ground on which to judge a work of art, almost as bad as judging it on the uses to which it is put. The greatness of *Othello* is not undermined by the violence done to Desdemona, nor by Shakespeare's possibly unenlightened view of race; the energy, the seemingly naive joy, of *Carmina Burana* is not made suspect by its premiere in the Germany of 1937; Emil Nolde's membership in the Nazi party does not vitiate the mystical power of his greatest paintings.[40]

Any artwork that makes us think and consider and feel deeply about life has at least some good in it. If a treatment is found to be inadequate beyond a certain point, then the question of art does not arise. The work can be seen to be either propaganda or trash, and thus worthy of condemnation, and may even become legitimate material for suppression. Thus, we might ban Ernst Zundel, but never Ezra Pound and Louis-Ferdinand Céline, and certainly not William Shakespeare.[41]

Who decides between art and propaganda, between art and "trash"? Those who inform themselves about it, those who argue about it with love for the subject. Above all there must be discussion, which means honest arguments, not harassment or suppression of artworks by groups determined to control the communication between a given creator (or institution) and the public. The arts flourish best in an atmosphere of free expression; if the artist chooses a political agenda, that is one thing, but to demand that he or she do so – or to object to an artwork solely on the basis of its political agenda – is quite another.

In the 21st century, if Canadian art is held hostage by political interests, if our art is required to reflect and amplify ideological imperatives (including nationalistic ones), then it will be finished as a living force. I do not think, however, that this will happen. I have faith – perhaps too great a faith – that common sense, a truer vision, will prevail.

6 The Nature of the Crisis

Support for Canadian culture is not declining through any con-
scious act of public will. Rather it is declining by a kind of apa-
thetic consent — the flagship, tossed for too long on heavy economic
seas, is in danger of foundering because not enough people care any
more to plug the leaks.
          — Max Wyman, Vancouver *Province*

FEDERAL GOVERNMENT INTERVENTION, in the form of financial support, more than any other factor, changed the cultural face of Canada. As we move into the next century, it is the failure of government action — the hesitations, confusions, and half measures of successive national governments — that threaten the creative development of that culture. And "action" is the relevant word. In a country where inquiries and surveys initiated by individuals, arts groups, institutions, and governments at all levels have resulted in a huge amount of expertise (much of it brilliant, creative, and still relevant), there should be no excuse for inaction on some of the pressing issues that challenge us in the nineties.

Then why is action not forthcoming? Is the notion of a "crisis" in our arts and culture unfounded, or is the term itself too exaggerated? Don't we notice everywhere in Canada the signs of thriving arts and culture? Have our cultural institutions been spoiled by years of lavish funding? Are our culture producers hopelessly inefficient? Actually there is plenty of evidence of waste and inefficiency — but they might be found in organizations in every sphere of activity, including in many universities, hospitals, and successful businesses. The whole picture must include not only a sense of the huge growth in the cultural sector (more artists, more companies) but also a look at funding cuts, rising costs, and a nonexpanding market: the result has been a dangerous, but perhaps hardly fatal, setback in the expected development of many of our arts groups.

Nonetheless many observers are pessimistic. In a 1995 interview with Pamela Wallin, Pierre Berton spoke of the ongoing assimilation and "Disneyfication" of Canadian culture, though he argued that "something" of our culture might survive, thanks especially to our flourishing literature. In a *Globe and Mail* article, Don McKellar, a screenwriter and actor, was quoted as sounding a kind of death knell, speaking about "the end of a lot of things. . . . It's really changing people's attitudes about the arts. We have to get money elsewhere [than from the Ontario or federal governments]. There's an unprecedented pessimism, timidity, about the arts."[1]

The first half of the nineties had already begun to reveal signs of trouble. Newspaper headlines about the arts, usually bland or celebratory, began to sound alarming: "A Downward Cultural Spiral," "Culture in Crisis," "Arts Going Down the Drain," "Funding Crisis at the Canada Council," "Performing Arts Companies Singing the Subscription Blues," "Telefilm Funds in Freeze Frame," "Situation précaire aux Grands Ballets Canadien," "Liberals Have Betrayed the CBC with Cuts," and so on.[2] These headlines were typical; at the same time, feature stories and editorials that sought the roots of the problem usually focused on the question of underfunding; or, more rarely, they sounded the lament that, despite the obvious health of our culture, audiences were not growing in proportion.

Given the failure of successive federal governments to revivify arts policy, and the spotty record of some of the new provincial administrations (most of which soon became obsessed by budget cutting), one could hardly expect our major cultural institutions to expand during the late eighties and early nineties. In fact, as the headlines I have cited show, they suffered one crisis after another, and observers began to think the unthinkable, that some of them might close down for good.

The situation was particularly bad for a few of the major symphony orchestras, notably those of Toronto and Vancouver, and for some of the leading dance companies, including the National Ballet of Canada and the Royal Winnipeg Ballet.[3] Stratford and many other theatres suffered.[4] Money was short, drastically so in some cases, and audiences were not increasing. Onstage, Gilbert and Sullivan and Broadway shows had to come to the rescue of Shakespeare and Ibsen and Tremblay. The creation of blockbuster special-effects musicals requiring the pooled resources of two or more theatres seemed to threaten the eventual demise of the smaller, more experimental regional groups. In addition to being yet another front for the invasion of popular culture, these musicals foreshadow a future domination of the theatrical scene by theatres in our largest population centres; this concentration, in turn, would do nothing to maintain the diversity of playwrights, actors, and technicians that has made the theatrical scene in Canada so exciting over the past few decades.

The major museums and galleries did not face large crises (with the notable exception of the Art Gallery of Ontario, roughly handled by the NDP's Karen Haslam), and some huge building projects reached completion, including the Museum of Civilization and the new National Gallery of Canada in Ottawa. Yet every museum and gallery wrestled with the question of how it could fulfill its institutional mission and not either offend its patrons or bore them to death; political correctness began to affect the choice of exhibitions, and a tendency toward sideshow vulgarity, or superficiality, emerged. Controversies over specific works (which can be healthy) sometimes revealed new depths of public ignorance of, and indifference to, art.

On another front, the publishing industry, transformed (as I have already indicated) by more than a decade of takeovers and other restructurings, has been kept busy trying to adapt to the new technology and to new market conditions. In the first half of the nineties, prominent Canadian publishing firms continued to go under, and the battle to have the GST removed from reading was lost; in effect, this tax withdrew nearly $100 million from the industry.[5] Propped up by federal help, Canadian publishers nonetheless originated approximately 80 percent of Canadian-authored titles (the sum of which, however, comprised only about 17 percent of the total book sales in Canada).[6] Yet all publishers, concentrating on nonfiction, prizewinning writers, and genre novels, have grown even more indifferent to fledgling creative work (especially to Canadian writers who have no immediate international potential), while the small presses, often nepotistic and narcissistic, though also intermittently inspired, showed the negative side of government dependency by kowtowing to the idol of political correctness.[7]

In November 1995 Borders Group, Inc., the giant American book retailer, announced plans to open its first Canadian superstore in Toronto. It was necessary to find Canadian partners to do this, because federal government policy requires that all ends of the book business have majority Canadian ownership and control. The announcement was greeted with alarm by Chapters, Inc., Canada's largest retail book chain (an amalgam of Coles and SmithBooks, which has some 400 stores coast to coast).[8] Clearly, if the American firms enter the market, Chapters would have to face stiff new competition. (Some small Canadian booksellers, having received little sympathy for losses incurred in their own battles to survive against the Canadian giants, were less than sympathetic to Chapters.)

At the same time, Jack Stoddart, chairman of Stoddart Publishing, and others expressed the fear that the Canadian retail book industry could not survive the American competition.[9] They suggested that Canada's delicately balanced book distribution system would be disrupted – Canadian publishers would lose this reliable source of income, because the newcomers would ignore the distribution rights that Canadian publishers have negotiated, or do an end run around them. The currently weak copyright laws could not protect Canadian interests, many asserted. A *Globe and Mail* editorial pooh-poohed such fears, suggesting that the new American firms would be unlikely to attempt to circumvent the Canadian middlemen.[10] But even if the American booksellers did begin to import books directly from the United States, the *Globe and Mail* maintained, this is no reason to suppose that Canadian publishers would cease to publish Canadian books. Jack Stoddart, on the other hand, referred to the example of the film industry, wherein the American grip on distribution makes it difficult for Canadian films to obtain a proper showing.

The federal government, for its part, has promised that a new and effective copyright law would protect Canadian firms from losing control of books they have negotiated to distribute.[11] At the same time, federal sources are insisting, in private, that the American chains hold to their tacit agreement to buy from Canadian distributors. A moderate form of protectionism, it might be said, won the first battle, but the war is hardly over. The Americans have made some concessions in order to gain entry into the market, but once they do, things may change rapidly and become irreversible. In light of this, one might ask whether Canadian publishers such as Stoddart are right, or whether the *Globe and Mail*'s rosy vision of the future can be believed.

Unfortunately there is probably more reason to accept the negative view. The fact that Canadian financial interests are involved in the new stores is irrelevant to the issue of Canadian content. Also, as the *Globe and Mail* itself admits, the Canadian middlemen are not legally protected; the American bookstores might well strike separate distribution deals with American distributors (especially because the Canadian distributors, as booksellers have repeatedly told me, are often less efficient). Finally it seems naive to assume, as the *Globe and Mail* editorial did, that Canadian books will find their way into bookstores no matter what. The threatened demise of many more small bookstores will shrink the shelf space for small press books in particular, no matter how worthy they are. The large American chains will be under pressure from American publishers to stock and promote more American books. The financial losses to Canadian publishers resulting from loss of distribution rights, which may occur despite promised safeguards, will hardly encourage them to publish more Canadian books; it will simply make them more financially vulnerable and more likely to gravitate to least common denominator material, much of which will come from south of the border. In other words, Jack Stoddart's comparison with film distribution doesn't seem so far-fetched.

Taken together, these shocks and changes in our arts production and distribution changed the consciousness of many artists and administrators, publishers and promoters, who had grown up expecting the expansive times to last forever. Suddenly they were thrown back much more fully on their own resources; they had to face the fact that in times of stringency one of the first things that households cut back on is the "luxury" of the arts, and the fact that the educational system had done very little, during the years of its supposed prosperity, to produce young people who might grow up to support (or even comprehend) the traditional aesthetic culture.

What about the artists themselves, the key figures in the estimated 600,000 or more "cultural workers" in Canada?[12] Have they been expecting too much? In fact, fairly recent figures show that the average annual income of an artist in Canada is about $12,000 – if we consider only income from artistic work.[13] This low figure reminds us that the federal government's per capita spending on the arts falls considerably short of that of other Western democracies; Canadians pay only something like four dollars a year, for example, to support Canada Council funding.[14] Even so the money available to help artists is decreasing; the chances now of getting a Canada Council grant for a project are not as good as they were a few years ago (see chapter 8).

Despite these realities it is increasingly clear that the issue is *not* merely one of funding. While cash may heal some wounds (for arts institutions as for all of us), the closer one looks the more one senses a deeper malaise in our cultural life, of which the less than exciting growth of our audiences is only a superficial indicator.

Consider. The Canada Council is suffering not only a financial crisis but also a crisis of morale. It is now clear that over the past decade it has been steadily declining as a force in promoting Canadian culture. Apart from underfunding there have been administrative wobbles, such as the unconsummated reunion with the Social Sciences and Humanities Research Council of Canada (a reunion rejected by the Senate in 1993) and, above all, the dramatic and seemingly unthought-out dismantling of the Art Bank and the Explorations Program in 1995. Relations between the Council and regional arts groups have been marked by tensions: the Council's long-standing effort to work on behalf of national unity (an unacknowledged agenda that perhaps should have been more honestly avowed) has done very little, it seems, to convince Quebec artists to veer away from separation. Artists in English Canada have either felt neglected (in the Maritimes or British Columbia) or been alarmed (in Ontario) at some of the Council's unfocused responses to the new arts politics, while artists of all regions have deplored what they regard as the Council's failure as an instrument of advocacy with the federal government.[15] And minorities have not been placated even by the Council's extraordinary attempts to defuse the issue of cultural bias.

The Council's major shift of policy accompanying the drastic (and self-inflicted!) 1995 budget cuts was announced in a document entitled "A Design for the Future" (it sounded more like a renunciation of the past). This "design" was formulated as a fait accompli at the highest levels of the Council; there was no general consultation with experienced administrators at midlevel, who remained mostly unclear as to why these particular goals were being pursued. Previously there had been only token consultation with arts groups, yet it was noisy tokenism: the new Council chair, Donna Scott, was savaged in public forums, and turned her own anger on artists in several contentious meetings.[16]

"A Design for the Future" was not only awkwardly presented but also raised some deeper questions about the Council's direction, and about its position vis-à-vis both the government and the artistic community. While there might have been a case for separating the Art Bank from the Council, the implications of the decision to cut it loose seem not to have been thought through. At one stroke the world's largest art-distribution program was endangered; months of meetings have followed in an attempt to decide what to do with the collection, and to determine what kind of program might fill the void left by the Council's seemingly peremptory decision. Despite the obvious need for trimming administrative expenses at the Art Bank, one would think that the Council would have been anxious to preserve some kind of purchase and distribution system (the "design" document talks about distribution as a key element in future arts policy). The succeeding consultations suggest a somewhat panicky attempt to preserve something of the Art Bank – yet by its hasty actions, the Council threatened the useful continuation of any part of the program. In addition, while the document trumpets "access" for artists, the Council was busy killing its most comprehensive access program, namely Explorations, surely the most imaginative and democratic arts-awards program ever to run in Canada.

Having initially botched the transformation and/or dismantling of the Art Bank, the Council stumbled again when the Art Bank Transition Advisory Committee, headed by former federal mandarin Arthur Kroeger, made its report in late November 1995. This 18-member committee, which had been hastily formed to deal with the administrative crisis induced by the Council's own precipitous actions, was a prestigious and knowledgeable one, staffed by gallery directors, artists, and by experienced Art Bank personnel.[17] Kroeger's committee recommended that the Art Bank remain connected with the Council, but that its management be contracted out, while a smaller staff, located in more modest premises, should aim, after a short transition period, to make the Art Bank self-supporting. The committee suggested that the Art Bank might offer works more than 10 years old to community colleges, hospitals, libraries, et cetera, while the remaining works and newly acquired art would be rented to an expanded clientele, including not only government, but small businesses, lawyers, and other members of the public.[18]

In common with widespread arts community opinion, and although the Council first announced the "phasing out" of the Art Bank, Kroeger's committee saw no reason why the bank should be closed, suggested that closure could only be damaging to Canadian artists and culture, and saw no responsible way in which the collection as a whole could be dismantled.

The response of Council chair Donna Scott and director Roch Carrier (in the form of a letter released with the report itself) was a curious one, bordering on indifference and even hostility.[19] Admittedly the report argued for a new budget of $1.2 million for the Art Bank, but excluded any allocation for promoting the collection to new clients. Yet the Scott-Carrier notion that the report made "unsubstantiated assumptions about the potential for rental income" seems absurd in the light of the Art Bank's past record in renting out its collection and given the success of the comparable rental program of the Australian Art Bank, cited by Kroeger. Council management also complained about the failure of Kroeger's committee to consider moving the Art Bank to a city closer to the proposed new markets, and once again raised the spectre of what would happen if much of the Art Bank's 18,000-piece collection were suddenly dropped into the somewhat shaky Canadian market for contemporary art.

That Scott and Carrier could respond so unhelpfully to a report produced by their own carefully chosen committee seemed further evidence of bad planning, policy uncertainty, or worse. At best it may have indicated a desperate playing for time in a crisis situation, ironically one of Council management's own making. How the Council decisions on the Art Bank and its response to the Kroeger Report can be reconciled with the declared intention of its strategic plan to put a new emphasis on the distribution of art across Canada is not clear.

In all this one can be forgiven for suspecting the worst, namely that Council managers were so eager to demonstrate to their government "masters" that they were capable of fiscal responsibility that they acted irresponsibly in chopping programs without fully consulting the arts community and without considering the down-the-road implications of their actions. If this is so, then the arm's-length principle on which Council "objectivity" depends can be seen to have been put in jeopardy, just as seriously as it had been with the political meddling attendant upon the "appropriation of voice" controversy. Not everyone at the Council or the Art Bank approved of the new policies put forth by upper management, and thanks to firings, transfers, and almost random shifts of portfolios, internal (staff) morale at the Council has been weakened both by cynicism and by a measure of despair about the future of all its programs.

Meanwhile Telefilm Canada, the other major arts-supporting institution, its five-year budget drastically cut in the early nineties, has been at the centre of a long-simmering conflict between Quebec and English-Canadian filmmakers. In English Canada there has been resentment over the dominant Quebec presence in the institution (Quebec receives 40 percent of the total budget, and Telefilm is "staffed from top to bottom mostly by Quebecers"), while within Quebec the attitudes to this federal presence in the cultural sphere have been predictably ambiguous.[20] Over the years the most central cultural issue at Telefilm has been how to balance commercial interests with the mission of producing art. Unfortunately the notion that Canadian culture in general is under siege has not caused the federal-provincial issue to recede in importance. A national film-funding body located in Quebec and largely staffed by Quebecers during the heady years of Quebec nationalism was bound to run into difficulties in convincing the public and professional filmmakers of its priorities. In fact, the issue ought to be resolved by reaffirming Telefilm as an instrument of Canadian national policy; there might have to be regional quotas for the distribution of funds, to ensure balance, especially if the headquarters remains in Montreal and the Quebec separation movement does not die away. Should Quebec ever separate, Telefilm Canada would surely be one of the casualties, yet either separation or "devolution" might mean that the province would simply take it over. Canada nonetheless needs such an agency if it is to maintain its cultural integrity. As for the NFB, which has recently been criticized for having "top-heavy management and an inept bureaucracy," its days seem numbered no matter what happens.[21]

That most prominent of our major national cultural "operating bodies," the CBC, has been experiencing a rocky passage in the mid-nineties, resulting not only from funding uncertainties but also from swiftly unfolding technological changes that affect the very nature of broadcasting, and from an unresolved debate about its role in Canadian culture.

The issue of CBC Television (in which direction should it go?) has been left unresolved by successive governments, while CBC Radio seems to be shamefully undervalued.

The federal government has attempted to address the crisis in various ways, namely through the parliamentary Standing Committee on Canadian Heritage, which delivered a (very tentative) report in June 1995; through the appointment of Perrin Beatty as president, to succeed the embattled Tony Manera; and through the creation of a commission headed by former CBC president, Pierre Juneau, which reported in January 1996, not only on the CBC, but on Telefilm Canada and the NFB.

While the reevaluation process continues, massive cuts that may involve as many as 3,000 jobs, the slashing of production teams at such quality programs as *Man Alive,* and the threatened cancellation of Radio Canada International have left CBC personnel and advocates of the corporation as a public broadcasting medium reeling.[22]

To many, such radical changes seemed premature in the absence of a comprehensive new mission plan for CBC. The *Globe and Mail,* in a November 23 editorial, following on the announcement of major downsizing ($67 million from English and $35 million from French television; $16 million from English-language and $13 million from French-language radio), outlined the kind of fundamental decisions that would have to be made. It suggested that the CBC should cut sports and local programming, switch to cable broadcasting, drop advertising, and become 100 percent Canadian.

There seems little doubt that, over the years, the CBC has grown to be an unwieldy bureaucracy, with too many highly paid executive producers, too much middle-level management, and administrators who are often noted for the pompous inanity with which they charge forth in defence of the status quo. It has been argued that if one were simply starting the whole corporation from scratch, one could do so for a mere $800 million or so; whereas rational trimming of the present $1 billion plus budget seems to offer endless problems. Radio is relatively cheap ($235 million) and successful, yet it is to take 17 percent of the proposed cuts, compared with the 12 percent for TV. Executives (and, reportedly, the Juneau Commission) are obsessed with TV. It is reported that they do not want to give up sports broadcasting (which brings in revenue – though the *Globe and Mail* casts doubt on how much sports broadcasting is really worth). Certainly prime-time sports seems hardly part of the mission of a public television operation, and Applebaum-Hébert had already suggested that CBC Television get out of "excessive" sports broadcasting in the early eighties.

With the corporation virtually under siege, we are experiencing a period of utter timidity in experimentation, even on radio, which in the past has often been inventive and challenging. Local CBC Radio (news and features) is highly regarded in many communities, yet the corporation seems to take it for granted, while the stereo FM network is a cultural bastion. If there is still much to be grateful for in radio programming, there is also room for improvement; what is obvious is a lack of real imagination in many of the current offerings. The approach taken to culture on the national FM network is often too chummy and "knowing" in the wrong way, or sometimes fuddy-duddyish. It could be more inventive, more informative; the arts commentary, which surely ought to incorporate new voices from all over the country, is mostly provided by a few selected old hands, or depends upon the limited perspectives of a narrow Toronto-approved circle.[23]

I fail to see how a solution to the CBC situation can be isolated from an overall cultural plan, which appears more and more to be needed, and of which there is as yet none in sight. If the expected cuts occur without an intelligent and practical restructuring, preferably including a visionary plan for the future of television, the corporation may never recover. The morale at the CBC is clearly at the lowest point in its history.[24]

The options put forth for changing the corporation include simply cutting back budgets and retaining most of the present programming, targeting some expensive areas and replacing them with cheaper productions, and making core changes that would involve a CBC withdrawal from certain areas of broadcasting altogether.[25] One of the large questions is: are the right people making decisions that will affect Canadian culture in such a comprehensive way over the next decades? Former heritage minister Michel Dupuy, who was ultimately responsible, seemed to have little input. Perrin Beatty, who has some strong credentials, has a record of connections with private broadcasting and a background in Brian Mulroney's cabinet. The CBC's 15-person board of directors (mostly lawyers, businessmen, accountants) includes 11 appointees from the Mulroney era.[26] Why is there not a broader representation of the Canadian public in the decision-making process? The CBC is surely the Canadian cultural institution that has the most loyal and enthusiastic following among the public. It has strong and longtime advocacy from such groups as the Friends of the CBC, while a Save the CBC campaign, including a coalition of public interest groups and individuals, was launched with the help of some important Canadian artists in November 1995.[27] These groups and individuals are not unaware of the financial necessities, yet they know that if the changes taking place do not result in a strong public broadcasting presence in Canada, much that we value in our Canadian heritage will be lost. John Haslett Cuff, the television columnist for the *Globe and Mail,* summed up the situation with brutal frankness. "The destruction of the CBC," he writes, "is perhaps the most symbolically important measure of the federal government's abrogation of responsibility, a clear sign that Prime Minister Jean Chrétien and his cabinet colleagues have given up the idea of Canada as a nation. And the poor leadership and misdirection that has crippled the CBC over the past decade is a direct result of successive federal governments' lack of commitment to, and understanding of, public broadcasting."[28]

The various problems and crises of the National Arts Centre (NAC) have naturally attracted less attention than those of the CBC or the Canada Council, though the centre is hardly less demoralized, and despite several major attempts to give it a more dynamic role, it has never been – since the early phase of the director-generalship of Donald MacSween in the late seventies – a significant part of the national arts consciousness. (The criticism that the NAC took from the country-wide arts community in those days indicated a certain measure of puissance; no one today would dream of kicking this poor, tired, old horse.) The administration of Yvon DesRochers in the early nineties (he was fired in 1994) was marked by controversy, administrative mudslinging, and an almost complete lack of artistic excitement.[29] To indicate the absurd depths to which the federal government is capable of descending in search of a solution for what has become another of its cultural white elephants, following DesRochers there was talk of attempting to lure Garth Drabinsky to the post of director general![30] That Drabinsky's undoubted talents have very little to do with the notion of culture that created the NAC in the first place is simply another indication of the confusion and loss of direction that afflict federal arts policy.

In December 1995, barely a year after her appointment as NAC director general, Joan Pennefather unexpectedly resigned. She had come into conflict with the NAC's board of directors over a new programming plan, one that would have featured "festival" presentations designed to replace the regular NAC season. This new concept, the board felt, had been too hastily conceived and had little chance of success, artistic or financial (at least within the time frame allotted).[31] Pennefather, for her part, seemed anxious to achieve a balance between the artistic and commercial sides of the operation, and had been proceeding cautiously, although there may well have been pressure from some board members to free more dates at the NAC for commercial presentations. Information was spotty, because board chair Jean Thérèse Riley baulked at open disclosure of any policy disagreements or financial uncertainties that had led to the scrapping of the new program and to the resignation of the director general, from whom much had been expected. This most recent NAC crisis once again raised questions about the administrative structure of the organization and demonstrated that ad hoc solutions to arts crises will usually fail. At the same time, one caught a glimpse of an unsavoury managerial elitism, which refused to disclose its real intentions and insisted that arts groups, not to mention the community at large, must simply take it on faith that their interests are being served by crucial decisions that are made in secret. Obviously a refashioning of the administrative structure of the NAC, and the creation of a new role for it within the context of a national arts policy, is more urgent than ever.

The next director general will have the major job of not only dealing with a strong-minded board, but will be taking over an institution about which few seem to care, but which carries a budget that, though constantly shrinking, still approaches the $15 million mark annually. Clearly revivification must be more than a matter of good administration and budget cutting; a creative plan involving some kind of nationwide mandate for the NAC is essential. This might take the form of the reestablishment of resident arts groups with a national constituency, or it might mean linking the NAC and its resident artists to a national arts network.

The CRTC – thanks to its regulatory function, almost always in the thick of controversy – has been consistently under pressure in the nineties. A new broadcasting law (1991) only seemed to increase the bureaucratic complexity of its operations, while substantive issues have come to the fore.[32] Cultural critics have continued to point out the absurd nature of some regulations concerning "Canadian content" (a Canadian soloist and a fully Canadian orchestra recording a foreign piece in Los Angeles does not qualify, nor would they qualify if they recorded the same piece for a foreign label in Winnipeg!)[33] The "consolidations" noticed everywhere in the communications industry (see chapter 2) have affected cable; the Bell colossus has begun to battle the specialized companies for control of this lucrative market. The three dominant English-language cable companies have been delivering 96 percent foreign drama and entertainment; the new, culturally oriented cable services have continued to disappoint, and questions have been raised about the failure of the CRTC to "milk" the broadcasting profits of the major players in order to create funding for new Canadian cultural programming, clearly a missing factor in all the hype about a new "arts" component on cable.[34]

Failed opportunities? A sense of decline? If we look past the central institutions and regulatory bodies to the parliamentary and cabinet levels, we find a number of years of disappointingly vague policies in cultural affairs. Brian Mulroney's government seemed at a loss as to how to deal with culture, indicated by its funding irrationalities (they were not all bad) and by its appointment of Felix Holtmann as chair of the Standing Committee on Communications and Culture. Marcel Masse, seen as a promising minister, lost much of his credibility by advocating an expensive and seemingly pointless Institute for Research on Cultural Enterprises in Montreal, a proposal that was quickly shelved after opposition developed on all fronts.[35] Remarkably unrevealing inquiries into the National Gallery of Canada's exhibition of Jana Sterbak's *Vanitas* and its purchase of Barnett Newman's *Voice of Fire* did little to reassure those who felt that the federal government was wasting its time on relative trivia while failing to deal with deep-seated problems.[36]

On the other hand, it has been Jean Chrétien's government that has dealt what has been perceived as the unkindest blow to the CBC; it has been under the Liberal appointees that the Canada Council has suffered its crudest shocks of change. Sheila Copps, who recently replaced the ineffective Michel Dupuy, presides over an unwieldy entity called, at last look, Canadian Heritage, a catchall name that in its vagueness probably symbolizes and sums up the bafflement of successive post-Trudeau governments about how to treat culture and the arts. (The Trudeau era had its blind spots as well, of course.)

Thus, despite the correct estimate of writers such as John Ralston Saul that our culture has never been so diverse, so rich, so worthy of the attention of all Canadians (and of the world), there is (both at the production level and in government circles) much doubt, confusion, disappointment, and downright pessimism. Although one can target the various federal governments for their lack of vision and commitment, my view is that many of the uncertainties are systemic; they derive from the fact that we have reached the end of one era in our cultural development but have not yet found a way to the next. We may well have entered what might be called "the second phase" of our postwar cultural growth without really acknowledging or taking on the challenges that derive from this fact.

The first phase began with the Massey report and resulted in the dynamic, diverse, thriving arts and cultural life that we see around us today. Our present sense of dissatisfaction, confusion, and groping results from the fact that we have established no clear path from this point. The Federal Cultural Policy Review Committee of 1980-82 (Applebaum-Hébert) in retrospect looks like a timely but somewhat uncertain attempt to prune and shape the growth established after the first (Massey-inspired) cultivation of the Canadian "bush garden" alluded to by Northrop Frye. While several of the key recommendations in the Applebaum-Hébert report were acted upon, many of its critics suggested that it failed to chart a consistent path for the future. Also, some of the real pressures on our culture emerged clearly only after it had concluded its inquiry.[37]

The end of the cold war saw the shifting of international attention to new economic alliances, communications and ecological issues, and the exchange of cultural and social initiatives. The latest technological leap ahead by means of computers and new broadcasting technology has changed the situation for every national culture. Under the Mulroney administration, the federal-provincial balance tilted considerably toward the provinces, and this process seems ongoing. The new Canadian mosaic, its complexity and challenges, the issue of multiculturalism versus mainstream culture – these have become sensitive areas that few politicians care to meddle with, while chronic budgetary woes at all levels of government have made policy decisions even more critical – and difficult. Clearly, as we head for the 21st century, our cultural policymakers, our institutions, and our artists are having to deal with complexities undreamt of by either Massey or Applebaum and Hébert.

At such a time it is probably inevitable that the various interested parties – governments, institutions, artists, analysts – will propose solutions in line with their fundamental convictions about the role of the arts in society. Those obsessed with abstract or specific notions of "free enterprise," or in love with the notion of the "independent artist," will propose doing away with the huge support structures that have been created since the Massey report; or perhaps, as in the recent policy announcements of Mike Harris's Conservative government in Ontario, they will suggest a movement away from unilateral government support and into "partnership" arrangements with the private sector. Nationalists will demand an encompassing guarantee of survival, even if this guarantee means going against present tendencies to cut and slash all "nonessential" state services. Artists who have protested the recent cutbacks, and who have become convinced that no further large-scale funding is forthcoming, will in many cases reassess their priorities and find innovative ways to continue to practise what is fundamental to their art. Special-interest groups will attempt to invoke principles of "equality" and "recompense for past injustices" to ensure that they retain some stake in future developments.

In order to measure the strengths and weaknesses of all such approaches (which suggest that the present system be pushed farther in one direction or another), we might focus on one of the more subtle and informed scenarios, that of John Ralston Saul, as outlined in the brief analysis of the cultural scene he wrote for the Department of Foreign Affairs in 1994. Saul is a nationalist with a strong vision of Canada's unique strengths; he points to our nonimperialist stance in world affairs, to our French-English mosaic, to our character as a "northern country." He denies that "globalization" of industries and communications networks, and financial cutbacks, create a hopeless situation for Canada. These latter two tendencies, taken together, in fact, create a fluid situation in which "there is a great deal of ground to be gained by a medium-sized nation willing to use its imagination and to build new international alliances based on practical shared interests."[38] Saul discounts the obsessive concern of many analysts with American culture and markets, and suggests that, while protecting and developing our internal cultural economy, we must look outward for markets and alliances, especially to Europe. He advocates no major structural changes in Canadian arts administration, believing that cooperation between arts groups and government at various levels can produce good results.

Saul's is clearly a well-thought-out and original approach, combining a sensible optimism with a shrewd sense of how the "game of culture" is played on the world stage. Nonetheless one might question whether the many-levelled and complex structure of arts "activators" in this country really provides a suitable base from which to put his ideas into effect. One might question, too, whether Saul doesn't underestimate the threat to Canadian culture from the "universal entertainment culture" largely created south of the border. If one suggests that we have "advantage Canada" whenever cultural material produced in this country is sold abroad, then there is little problem. But if one fails to distinguish between "produced in Canada" and "Canadian" (which I do not think is usually an arcane, elusive, or subjective distinction), then the point of Saul's argument seems blunted. No one doubts that Canada can get a part of the cultural action, but isn't it important (if we are to keep our culture alive) that the action we get be uniquely Canadian? (see chapter 4). It also seems to me that, lacking a strong profile, an agreed-upon mission, a recognizable "face," the arts and culture will never become an important element of either our domestic or our foreign agendas, despite the persuasive efforts of writers such as Saul.

All the solutions referred to above address the cultural crisis, but do not, I believe, go far enough in suggesting changes to the structures that produce and distribute culture in this country and abroad. The problem lies not merely in funding shortages or in pressures from a changing internal and external economy; we are at the point where our whole cultural system itself needs an overhaul. The trick is to accomplish this rejuvenation without reaching for impossibly radical solutions, to discover, in short, for the benefit of Canada's culture, a solution that, in terms of the Canadian psyche and the Canadian tradition of the "middle way," will ring true.

7 Artistic Culture: A Way of Renewal

The posture of governments vis-à-vis the arts is nowadays domi-
nated by the perception of the artistic community as a legitimate
and worthwhile element of society, not merely, as was the case earli-
er, as an infinitesimal minority of somewhat eccentric individuals.
The arts, artists and their followers have become part of the
Canadian mainstream and are recognized as such.
 – John Meisel and Jean Van Loon, "Cultivating the
   Bushgarden: Cultural Policy in Canada"

CANADIAN ARTS AND CULTURE deserve government support;
in some respects, indeed, they could hardly survive without it.
Yet the question remains: what kind of support can reasonably
be expected, given the economic, social, political, and technological
changes of the nineties and beyond?

Government support assumes the political will to make decisions that
will involve spending taxpayers' money. This will might be counted on if
Canadian artists and arts organizations successfully argued their case for
the arts, if the Canadian public really accepted the notion that art is an
essential service and therefore should be supported by the state.

Unfortunately, despite some notable attempts, this conversion of the
public to a belief in the arts and culture as an everyday necessity has never
been accomplished. I talk to people every day – good, ordinary, educated,
middle-class citizens – without any particular ideological convictions right
or left who are baffled by my concern over the survival of the arts and culture in Canada. They can understand a government providing education
and health services, maintaining prisons, an army, a postal service – but the
notion that the government should pay contemporary artists to create new
works appears incomprehensible to them. If you ask them if we should let
our symphony orchestras, our art galleries and museums, our ballet compa-

nies and great theatres, perish, they say that this would be undesirable, and they are generally willing to contribute dollars to make sure that it doesn't happen. But to pay *more* out of their own pockets to fund contemporary novelists, painters, composers? To most of the Canadian public, I'm sure, this is an unthinkable proposition, especially in times of financial shortfall.

The first thing any new arts policy has to accomplish, therefore, is general acceptance of a clear and powerful declaration of the place of the arts and culture in Canadian life. Artists, administrators, and government agencies must join forces to make clear the importance of art in our national development; they must state their objectives in a bold and memorable form and open permanent lines of communication with the ordinary public, with those citizens who are currently unconcerned with, or even hostile to, the arts.

Further on I will state a few points that ought to be included in any such declaration of artistic purpose. But first I want to make clear my general position on the question of arts reform, which is simply this: any changes we make cannot be radical; we must reform the system step by step, *in line with the reality of existing governmental structures and in terms of the financial realities faced by the country.*

For the sake of clarity, however, let me tackle this question point by point; let me begin at the beginning and ask two questions: (1) What should Canada do for its artists and its cultural sector? (2) What can the cultural sector and Canadian artists do for Canada?

The answer to the first question is that Canada should support culture and the arts because they are necessities of civilized life, and there can be no national identity, no national purpose, no historical memory, and no richness of life for our citizens without them. Culture is the most inspiring, the most provocative and creative form of national defence, that one can imagine. Canada should support arts and culture because our nation cannot survive as an integral and independent entity without them, and the cost of supporting them is minimal in relation to this result. This point must be conveyed to the general public, once and for all. Once this principle is established, it will be much easier to accept the notion that the state should give artists and cultural institutions the means not only to survive but also to grow, though it should be remembered that these means need not always involve direct financial assistance.

As for the second question (what can the cultural sector and artists do for Canada?), the *wrong* answer is that they should devote their efforts to promoting national unity, national survival, or to enhancing Canada's image in the world. The *right* answer is that *they should be themselves* – that is, *they should make art,* without fear of censorship by the government, the public, or their fellow artists. They should create, preserve, display, or market whatever art springs from the creative sources within them. Canadian artists should practise their art in a climate of freedom. They may celebrate life, or they may challenge us with new and disconcerting visions of reality, but the important thing is that they follow their creative impulses, which alone will guarantee the authenticity of what they make.

I have summarized the changes that I believe we should insist on, in order to deal with this second phase in our postwar cultural development, in the following seven headings.

I. ESTABLISH THE BASIC PRINCIPLES OF A NEW POLICY FOR ARTS AND CULTURE

In 1974 Sweden reformulated its cultural policy, listing eight points summarizing the general goals that a state cultural policy should strive to achieve.[1] These points underlay most subsequent legislation that dealt with arts and culture, and were at the centre of all debates about future activities in that sphere. Almost every point in the Swedish declaration is relevant to the Canadian situation, and I will therefore list them here, with some editorial changes and additions designed to meet the needs of Canada's present cultural situation. It would not be so difficult to produce a cultural "bill of rights" from the principles below, and as I noted at the beginning of this chapter, this is, in my opinion, an essential step. (It should be remembered that the ordinary Canadian grows up in an environment far less enriched with cultural artifacts and memories than his or her European counterpart. Stating the obvious is therefore not a bad way to begin promoting culture.) Throughout this book I address the question: *why culture?* (see, especially, my concluding observations). This question should be the first part of any cultural bill of rights, but once we have answered it, we must address the concomitant issue: *what should cultural policy accomplish?* And here the Swedish example is eminently useful.

1. Cultural policy should help to protect freedom of expression and create genuine opportunities for its exercise. This will be accomplished in many ways, but absolutely fundamental are the principles that granting agencies should maintain an arm's-length distance from any government, and that censorship of the arts in any form is unacceptable.

2. Cultural policy should give people opportunities to engage in creative activities of their own in their own communities. It should recognize that though technology may assist in the creation and promotion of culture, culture is not always furthered by improvements in technology.

3. Cultural policy should counteract the negative effects of commercialism in the cultural sector.
4. Cultural policy should promote a decentralization of funding and of decision-making functions in the cultural sector.
5. Cultural policy should make allowance for the needs of disadvantaged groups of all kinds.
6. Cultural policy should facilitate continuous artistic and cultural renewal.
7. Cultural policy should ensure that the culture of earlier times is preserved and revitalized.
8. Cultural policy should promote Canada's national culture in the international sphere and welcome exchanges of culture with other nations where such exchanges do not threaten the survival of our national culture.

With these principles firmly in view, we can ask ourselves what major structural changes (in government, in funding) are necessary to take Canada confidently into the next century.

II. CREATE A MINISTRY OF CULTURE

Canada desperately needs a ministry to deal exclusively with cultural affairs. It would be absurd to try to create and administer policy for the armed forces without a Department of National Defence; it is equally absurd to attempt to organize, promote, and sustain the growth of our culture without a minister who is specifically responsible for this task. Even on the level of symbolism, the idea of a Ministry of Culture would offer us a potent image of national commitment to the arts and culture.[2]

It is instructive to look at a government handbook that outlines the duties assigned to the present Canadian heritage ministry. Transport, water power, fitness and amateur sport, manufacturing standards, superannuation – one wouldn't be surprised to find the ministry involved in tulip breeding, amateur juggling, or ESP. The list of responsibilities is long and complex and daunting, and the cultural functions divided among several bureaucracies. Confusing? Of course – in fact, an administrative impossibility. Anyone who examines the federal structures supporting culture, anyone who sees the diversity of agencies and departments involved, will immediately suspect a confusion of purpose, and will understand the difficulty of running consistent policies through such a diversity of administrative channels. Of course, one might argue that such "horizontal" decentralization is healthy. But given that the federal government's role in cultural affairs is both manifold and in practice often blurred and ineffective, we must assume the opposite; besides, the lines of responsibility are hardly clear. One part of the system often seems to work in ignorance of, or at cross-purposes with, another, and more important, it makes effective liaisons with the provincial governments an absolute nightmare of complexity. No wonder artists at the grass roots are dissatisfied, confused, yet unsure whom to blame.

The creation of a Ministry of Culture should be the first step in Canada's radical simplification and centralization of its arts administration. The ministry should include, as divisional entities, such components as the Canada Council and the Social Sciences and Humanities Research Council of Canada, the Public Lending Rights division, the heritage side of Canadian Heritage, the multicultural component, the various cultural industries sectors – in short, every unit that concerns itself with culture in the traditional sense – with print, performance, and artifact culture, as well as research units that specialize in traditional culture.

Under such an arrangement some things would change: the Canada Council bureaucracy would shrink; it would lose its duty of representing artists (which it does badly, anyway); and it would concentrate on supporting the key cultural producers in this country, shifting away from the distribution of individual grants, which would more and more devolve upon the provinces (see chapter 8). On the multicultural side, where there is even more wastage, and absurd doles, the government would cease giving grants to groups such as the United Irish Societies of Montreal, the Retired Black Miners, or the Lao Association of Manitoba, and would concentrate on assisting minorities, immigrants, and ethnic groups in making their own unique contributions to the cultural mainstream.[3] For example, instead of funding Ukrainian dance groups that simply re-create Old World rituals, it would fund (if they appear) creative integrations of such traditional dances with contemporary forms and practices. Multiculturalism would exist to encourage such transformations, and thus ensure the survival of the most creative elements of ethnic culture. It should not exist to preserve European or Asian customs in Canada.

In addition – and this is absolutely critical – an instrument would be added to the new ministry that would begin the decentralizing of cultural administration in areas where doing so would be advantageous. This group would open new and important lines of communication both within the traditional arts community and between the arts community, other cultural players, and the public (see IV below).

I can imagine at this point several groups of readers throwing up their hands in horror at the very notion of such a ministry.

First, we have the seasoned bureaucrats who, with their knowing smiles, will adduce a thousand reasons why the octopus cannot be replaced by something simpler, more effective. What happens to areas, such as fitness and amateur sport, or Parks Canada, that will be severed from the present monster? Do we create separate ministries for all the miscellaneous activities that we now fit so conveniently under the aegis of "heritage." I would respond with my own questions: do we really need a ministerial umbrella for all these activities? When was the last time cabinet-level representation was required for canal offices or the Atlantic national parks? Is the heritage ministry really doing a good job of representing them all?

Second, we have the artists who fear that a Ministry of Culture would either generate less support than the present multidimensional monster or be too subject to political control. I would argue that in the past decade funding has not been effective or generous; a ministry such as I suggest could only improve the situation. It would have a much higher profile and a clear mission: to preserve and promote Canadian culture, and to establish a better means of coordinating funding with the provinces.[4] As for the threat of censorship, we have a strong tradition of artistic freedom in this country, a tradition that could hardly be subverted by any such ministry. I also assume that the principles of cultural development listed above would form the "charter" for any changes, thus giving a written guarantee in perpetuity for Canadian artistic freedom.

When government structures relating to culture were created after the Second World War, Canada opted for the British-style arts council and rejected the French-style cultural ministry, but we should not take the British mode for an eternal and perfect form. The British were never really at home with the notion of culture; as a friend of mine put it, not entirely facetiously, they created arts councils to defend themselves from culture, rather than to protect the arts. Some have argued that a cultural ministry would threaten the independence of the arts community, that it would create an "official" culture. (As I have indicated earlier in this book, even the council concept has not prevented the government from trying to turn arts and artists to political uses.) Given the notion that a Ministry of Culture would be accompanied by a strong decentralization of arts administration, a cabinet-level ministry could be a most useful instrument for signalling to the public that cultural production is inseparable from national existence.

Which leads me to the third group of possible objectors, those with provincial interests, who will oppose the creation of a Ministry of Culture because it would endanger the decentralization of arts and culture that they mostly desire. On the contrary, one main reason for establishing the ministry would be to create a coherent interface between the

federal, provincial, and municipal levels. It is much easier to divide
responsibilities if we have sharply defined administrative lines. Right
now the lines are very blurred. A Ministry of Culture would exist not to
impose a homogenous culture on Canada but to give our diverse culture
a strong voice in the federal and international spheres, and to facilitate,
through means both structural and technological, the coordination of
local activities in the arts, so that the national *heterogeneity* would be visible from every point. In my opinion the creation of such a ministry
would be the best means of creating a new federal-provincial balance,
and would take us away from the notion that the federal government has
the overriding responsibility for culture.

Fourth, we have the technophiles, who are convinced that virtual
reality, multimedia performances, and other heavily technologized forms
of the arts represent the common art of the future; such critics would
consider the creation of a Ministry of Culture to be an example of
"rearview mirror" philosophy, such as McLuhan professed to despise. I
have taught futurology and have often noted the inaccuracy of even
some of the most "obvious" predictions; I suggest that prophecies of the
death of the traditional "live" arts are distinctly premature. I believe that
the performance of arts in the future will be quite other than the advocates of supertechnology imagine. I don't doubt that our future culture
will be heavily involved with the mass media, but unless live performance
survives, we may as well shut up our cultural departments (see chapter 3).

Fifth, we have the various groups with a strong stake in the present
multicultural funding. They should realize that such funding is bound to
wither away in the long run, and should be looking for ways to shift the
emphasis to a more creative contribution from ethnic cultures.

In short, the creation of a Ministry of Culture is a sensible and logical step that would help to carry us into the 21st century with a new face
and purpose for the arts and culture in Canada.

III. SEPARATE THE MINISTRY OF CULTURE FROM THE MINISTRY OF MASS COMMUNICATIONS, NEWLY CREATED

The whole apparatus of mass communications (now in the portfolio of
the minister of industry) should be properly and logically placed together in a new Ministry of Mass Communications. Communications are not,
as some would argue, merely "another industry," to be dealt with as part
of development strategies, interprovincial and international trade deals,
and commercial policies. Communications are the heartbeat, so to speak,
not only of the Canadian economy but also of the Canadian psyche and

identity; they are the means of articulating what we are to ourselves and to the world. Allowing communications issues that affect us all to become "invisible" within a framework of industrial and commercial strategies is in itself a great danger to our culture. Communications issues raise problems comparable in their own area to the problems raised by genetic manipulation in the sphere of biology, and to those raised by euthanasia in the medical sphere. As McLuhan famously pointed out, you cannot separate the content from the medium; we need to think through issues far beyond their commercial and technical aspects when dealing with communications. We need to be able to frame media questions in terms of larger questions. What kind of society do we want? Who will control what we see, hear, and access? What rights do individuals have in regard to the new media? How might traditional values, such as freedom of speech, be best safeguarded in the new media world? What areas of government, education, and general culture are suitable for media transformation, and where should we go slowly?[5]

Any new Ministry of Communications should take under its wing such culturally central agencies and institutions as Telefilm Canada, the NFB, the CBC, and the CRTC, though they would obviously operate at the arm's-length distance already established. Such a ministry would be ideal as an information centre and promoter of some of the less traditional art forms, especially those connected with technology – I mean various kinds of video, performance, and interdisciplinary art, most of which fit uncomfortably or not at all into programs that serve the traditional arts. (The Media Arts section of the Canada Council, for example, would be better placed in this new ministry.)

Separating communications from both industry and a more traditional cultural ministry does make sense in terms of efficiency, though I can already hear cries of "multiplying the bureaucracy"; I anticipate the argument that because the move toward superministries saved us millions, it would be foolish to return to the bad old days when ADMs were as common as logs in the Ottawa River near Parliament Hill. As a layman observing the situation, I don't quite comprehend why dividing up a pie should necessarily make it larger. We already have departments, bureaus, agencies, divisions – call them what you will – that deal with all the matters I refer to here. I am merely suggesting, that in the name of logic, clarity, and efficiency, we reorganize what we have.

I believe that with culture and communications clearly visible in two separate but mutually aware ministries, we could face the future with a much clearer sense of priorities in the vital areas of national identity, control of cultural resources, production and distribution of culture, and federal-provincial interaction in the sphere of culture. And what we would save on special commissions of inquiry, extraordinary reports, and Band-Aid solutions to deal with this crisis or that would more than make up for any temporary financial inconvenience.

Because the most sensitive plant in the whole hothouse of communications and culture is the CBC, a few words about the corporation may be in order. The CBC is a hugely expensive cultural operation, and the tendency, following upon the present reexaminations, will surely be to cut it and make it more cost-effective. There is nothing wrong with this approach, as long as it is understood that the whole apparatus of a national culture may be threatened without a strong television and radio component. This is true, even though we are entering an era of satellite broadcasts and multichannels, an era of almost unlimited viewer choice.

By the time this book is published, we will have been through another round of examination of the CBC, carried on through an external auditing process and the deliberations of the commission headed by Pierre Juneau, former CBC and CRTC head. Changes will no doubt be proposed, changes that might have been engineered more efficiently and cheaply from within a ministry with the responsibility of setting policy in this specific area. But any changes proposed by the current inquiry groups will, in my opinion, be in vain unless the following measures are assured.

Advertising should probably not be tolerated on CBC Radio or Television. Felix Holtmann, the former Tory chair of the Commons Committee on Communication and Culture, whose obiter dicta have become legendary, once asked Pierre Juneau, apropos of radio, "Why are you not throwing an advertisement in every once in a while to pay for that programming? If you advertised even a little, I think it would wake people up who were listening to these long, drawn-out musicians from another country. . . ."[6] If Holtmann had been able to listen to a station such as WQXR in New York (the *New York Times* radio station), he would have had a stronger case for combining advertising and culture on a quality radio service. Nonetheless my case rests.

Sane and strong Canadian-content regulations must be introduced for all broadcasting. At present only four percent of all English broadcast drama and entertainment on television is defined as Canadian. Means must be found to improve on this percentage and to ensure that such content is *truly* Canadian, but we need to get away from the absurdity of legalistic quotas. What we want is to create a public that looks forward to experiencing Canadian art. This means a service in which we are not constantly reminded that the content is Canadian, or non-Canadian. Above all we don't want to re-create with our mass media the situation that we often have at our orchestral concerts, in which a token Canadian piece is slipped in between Beethoven and Elgar, like some necessary purge to be endured in order to make contact with pleasurable traditions. The way to get away from this approach is to cluster the new and more difficult work in festivals and special presentations, which will please the enthusiasts, and to promote in a broader context the Canadian art that has wide appeal, in order to lead listeners gradually to the more experimental vehicles.

CBC Radio must be taken seriously, and not forgotten or displaced in the rush to reform television. We can only hope that the new shows are as fundamentally Canadian as *Morningside* and *As It Happens*; that there is high visibility for unique Canadian artists; that there is representation of our diverse culture, *without quotas*; that innovation is not conceived of as merely phone-in, issue-related talk shows, rock-nostalgia shows, or religious broadcasts that imitate and are indistinguishable from the American products.

Reconstruction of the CBC will be in vain, however, unless the heavily Torontocentric nature of present cultural broadcasting is altered; there must be a new emphasis on creating familiar regional voices. There should be a strong Quebec centre, and active production in Ottawa, Winnipeg, Calgary or Edmonton, Regina, Halifax, and Vancouver at the least. The role of aesthetic culture must be guaranteed, for therein lies a great strength of Canadian self-expression.

A television culture channel (the long-contemplated CBC-2) should be created.[7] This channel should be given generous production funds and a cultural mandate that ensures there will be no simple recycling of existing products (à la Bravo!).

CBC FM-stereo should certainly improve its reach into the cultural community. It should cease to be a cozy haven for a small number of "commentators" and "experts" who are paid to talk to one another in public (though some of them are very good). It is vitally important to create strong local production, to keep an open shop, and to use many freelancers and onetime commentators, in order to ensure that new voices will appear. It should not be a question of waiting to see how long it will be before some new "talent" in Winnipeg or Halifax is dragged off to perform in the Glenn Gould Studio. Good local talent should be induced to remain local, and this can happen if a decentralization of the arts scene in Canada takes place.

IV. CREATE, WITHIN THE MINISTRY OF CULTURE, AN ARTS
INFORMATION, EDUCATION, AND ADVOCACY DIVISION LINK-
ING THE FEDERAL GOVERNMENT AND THE PROVINCES

The Ministry of Culture should include an Arts Information, Education, and Advocacy Division, whose main mission would be to give artists and cultural field-workers a chance to make their ideas known to one another, to the public, and to administrators at all levels. One way that this could be accomplished is through the creation in each province of an instrument that would also be a main channel of federal-provincial exchange on cultural matters. We need a national network of arts expertise with its roots firmly planted in the local scene. To that end Cultural Education Councils should be established on the provincial level, but with a provision for federal representation. These councils should meet and communicate regularly on specific long-standing issues or discuss new ideas, proposals, and problems with their counterparts across the country. The agendas could be set both locally and nationally; they would be diverse and would cover, over a period of time, almost all aspects of the arts and culture. Representatives of provincial arts councils and education ministries, as well as of the federal Ministry of Culture, plus – and this is extremely important – teachers, artists, arts administrators, and other interested parties (depending on the issue dealt with) would be able to participate in such councils.

These "town meetings on the arts and culture" would guarantee a continuous federal-provincial dialogue; they would promote the exchange of ideas and programs, and provide a forum for fast-developing issues; they would put arts education on a solid footing, and work against the worst kind of isolation of the arts community.[8] This network should be, in fact, a national lifeline of cultural information and arts promotion. The various provincial meeting dates need not coincide or overlap, but the meetings should make use of the latest communications technology and the new information highway. Where necessary, translations would be made available to erase the language barrier. Thus, each council branch would remain local, yet have the benefit of nationwide expertise and input. This would be an important, even an essential, element in any responsible decentralization of the national culture.

The argument against this kind of arrangement today is that it will create yet another bureaucracy, which we can't afford. In fact, such an arrangement would create no bureaucracy at all and would not be costly. One- or two-day annual or semiannual meetings in each province (the face-to-face element is important), with links maintained in between by E-mail or other means, would suffice. Bureaucratic frills would be minimal, and the results of the exchanges could be made available immediately.

Let me give a few examples. If such groups existed, then the whole country would have access to information about creative new departures, such as the Winnipeg New Music Festival. Many observers have been struck by the success of this festival in attracting a new, large, and enthusiastic audience. While information about the festival is available, the process of obtaining it can be laborious and costly. When such breakthroughs occur, whether in marketing, organization, performance arts, or funding techniques, the new Cultural Education Councils would make such information instantly available to all parts of the country. Problems could be resolved, or at least aired, without reliance on secondhand sources. A Native Canadian artist in the Northwest Territories could communicate an issue affecting his local culture and make contact across the country. The councils could exchange information on developments in provincial arts funding. A Toronto publisher, a Saskatchewan teacher, a New Brunswick gallery owner – anyone with an innovative idea about arts creation or teaching or marketing would have a ready audience for it.

V. REFORM THE CANADA COUNCIL AND GIVE IT A NEW ROLE AS MONITOR OF OUR INDISPENSABLE CULTURAL INSTITUTIONS

The Canada Council's influence on the development of arts and culture in this country has been enormous and largely positive; however, the weight of its influence has been exerted through dispersal of grants and awards. And in recent years, of course, the federal government's commitment to provide endless largess for our ever-expanding cultural activities has been cast in doubt.

Even in its heyday the Council had serious weaknesses, which were never really corrected. The policy behind the distribution of grants has sometimes been puzzling, the jury system unsatisfactory (see chapter 8). What concerns me here, however, is the extent to which the Council has been divorced from the grass roots, on the one hand, and ineffective in speaking out for the arts and culture, on the other. The Council has almost completely failed as an advocacy body; its arm's-length distance from government, its status as a virtually independent agency, has hampered it in this regard. It has often seemed like an inexplicable alien body to many legislators – and, no doubt, to a few prime ministers. Certainly provincial ministers and federal MPs have often regarded the Council with suspicion, as a hatching house of cultural puzzles or embarrassments. It's a tribute to Canadian good faith, and perhaps to our national, deep-down indifference to both the arts and religion, that we have never seen a real attack on the Council to match the furious assault of the American religious right on the National Endowment for the Arts.[9]

Surely, however, we have come to a new point of departure. Under my plan the Council would not even attempt to contact grass-roots artists; they would be served by the provincial Cultural Education Councils, and members of these bodies would have the responsibility – and would be given the means – to speak from and for all the regions.

The Canada Council should be reformed and integrated into the administrative structure of the new Ministry of Culture. The clout available to the ministry would revive the power of the Council, which would be able to concentrate its attention on helping to preserve the "untouchables," the 20 or 30 national arts and cultural institutions without which Canada would hardly be Canada (see chapter 8). The Council would monitor and provide funding for these institutions.

Beyond this the Council might work toward a French-style "culture house" concept.[10] It would be useful to establish across Canada a chain of cultural centres, designated as such and drawing strength from each region, while maintaining national connections. Each community could take pride in these facilities, which would originate important works and exhibit or perform them and others from across the country and abroad. Such culture houses would in most cases not have to be built; many already exist – the NAC in Ottawa, for example, which was originally to have this role, but which has never really achieved it. Many existing facilities across the country could serve as part of this network, and though some of them lack flexibility of space and design, combining them with an alternative local space would often achieve greater flexibility. Tours of shows, exhibitions, and visits by dramatic performers and musicians would be integrated into a national network (and become part of the broadcast mission of CBC-2). Naturally this would still leave plenty of room for nonestablished, offbeat activities, which would continue to take place in small theatres, barns, church basements, and so on all across Canada. (Just try to stop them!) The Canada Council's present system of literary readings, to take one example, is costly and lacks coherence, while tours by Canadian orchestras and art exhibitions in this country are almost nonexistent. A chain of performing units would improve the situation; this is really what the Council should be working toward in its new emphasis on "touring."

In addition the Council must compensate for its thoughtless undermining of the Art Bank which, despite problems, played a useful role in our arts scene. As I write, discussions are being held at the Council in order to attempt to transfer some of the Art Bank's functions elsewhere, perhaps to the private sector. Cooperation between the public and private sectors is a good idea in this area, but the notion of simply "unloading" the Art Bank material, or of dispensing with its services altogether, seems absurd.[11]

VI. BEGIN TO DECENTRALIZE CULTURAL FUNDING AND ADMINISTRATION

Local culture production is strong in Germany and Sweden, and has been of increasing importance in France despite the traditionally centralized nature of that system.[12] Canadian municipalities lack the taxing and administrative power of those in Sweden, while the provinces lack the historic cultural density of the German Länder. Yet the provinces have been extremely active in cultural funding and production, support of institutions, et cetera.[13] Artists, on the other hand (particularly in the West), haven't seemed to trust the provincial governments, which often have a "populist" component and are thought to be mostly captive to the traditional rural indifference to art.[14] In the nineties all provinces are chiefly occupied with budget-cutting measures, which would seem to leave little place for the support of culture. It is important to realize, however, that the financial situation may improve in the provinces before it does on a national level; several provinces have strong commitments to the goals of fiscal responsibility. If this means simply cutting back support to areas such as education, health, and the arts, if true fiscal reform embodying new efficiencies and the generation of new revenues fails, then the arts as we know them will be mortally wounded, anyway. But if, as some argue, the move toward fiscal responsibility actually restores the power of the provinces to fund such things as education and the arts, then a decentralization of our cultural support systems will be essential. Reorganization of the whole apparatus of the federal government's cultural administration should surely factor in the possibility of allowing many of its functions to devolve eventually upon the provinces. The creation of a strong federal arts-information infrastructure (the provincial Cultural Education Councils, described above) will keep communication lines open and enable the provinces to make intelligent funding choices, to see regional priorities in terms of the national overview.

A healthy culture cannot be imposed from the top. It must spring from the grass roots, not for some mystical reason of race and blood, but because individual artists live and work in a particular place and often make contact with this fact in their work. How much better to have them judged, rewarded, and promoted by their fellow citizens locally than by some committee or jury purporting to represent national "consensus," or by some faceless agency in Ottawa!

Decentralization, however, also requires that provincial arts councils be effective bodies with distinct facilities for the support of culture. Several provinces lump culture with tourism in a way that denigrates its centrality; all provinces devote much of their "culture" budgets to supporting libraries and heritage projects – which are extremely valuable in themselves, but do not involve culture creation.

British Columbia and Quebec have, within the past few years, created their own provincial arts councils, modelled on the Canada Council, while Ontario has had a strong arts council since 1963. Quebec's support for culture has been impressive in some ways but, contrary to some opinions, very spotty in others, and the sad fact is that only about 40 percent of Quebecers actually consume their province's cultural products.[15] The recent strong threat of Quebec separation has pushed federal thinking even further in the direction of decentralization – designed to placate provincial interests – which was already under way in the Mulroney era. How much farther can we go without undermining the coherence of Canada as a nation? Obviously Quebec separation would be a disaster, yet if separation comes, it may be a slow and partial process. Cooperation of all kinds between an independent Quebec and Canada would continue. And in the sphere of culture and the arts, such cooperation would be essential because of the new vulnerability of a weakened Canadian union to American penetration. Language would isolate Quebec from the North American megapolitics, and given the long tradition of understanding and cooperation between English and French Canada (despite the problems!), given the integration of the two languages in our present national institutions, it would be absurd if there were no continuing union on the cultural front. This position may seem to be one that dissolves in irony, given the sense of many Quebecers that the main issue of separation is cultural survival; I would argue that whether separation occurs or not, the best route of cultural survival for both Quebec and Canada is through a strong umbrella agreement on culture that connects the former with the familiar, if rivalrous and sometimes alien, Anglo culture. This relationship, though it might be uneasy (as in the past), would make possible, in the long run, an overarching *Canadian* culture that immediately differentiates itself from the American national culture.

It is obvious that a system of regional support for culture will result in inequities, and I see absolutely no problem with that prospect. (It occurs in Sweden and Germany, for example.) It is up to each region, each province, to determine what support it will give to the arts, up to artists, dialoguing with one another through the federal-provincial councils and other media, to set priorities with a *local* flair. Provincial governments of whatever political persuasion will be far more likely to support the arts and culture if they are part of a national information and education network and have access to the latest ideas about the creation and development of art – and audiences. If Canadian artists continue to hold the view that Ottawa must stamp the arts with some kind of bureaucratic imprimatur, they will remain hostage to a failing system. A federal sanction is not necessary: let the people create from their own communities, and let provincial and federal governments give them the means to develop their own work and to discourse with other parts of Canada about it. Only then will we have a healthy cultural life in Canada.

The federal government, while it strengthens its own commitments to culture, and gives culture and the arts a stronger profile nationally and internationally, must be willing to increase the amount of cultural funding it disperses to the provinces. The example of the American National Endowment for the Arts, which (as of 1990) passed on nearly 30 percent of its appropriations to the states, is relevant. Transfer payments have always comprised a large proportion of provincial revenue; the establishment of a Ministry of Culture would enable cultural transfer payments to be rationalized, and would result in a trickling down of federal funding, not only to the provinces, which already have strong revenue sources, but even to the relatively indigent Canadian municipalities. (Some people predict an eventual end to all transfer payments; this would not be fatal for the arts if the provinces develop their own strong support systems, but the federal government must stay in the game in order to provide coordination, communication, and a national purpose.)

If the federal government, in cooperation with the provinces, can facilitate the efficient operation and survival of key institutions, if it can assist continuing coast-to-coast dialogue between artists, teachers, administrators, and the public, and if the successful artistic creations of one region can reach other areas of Canada, then artists have nothing to lose, and almost everything to gain, by a process of decentralization.

VII. INCREASE THE CULTURAL VISIBILITY OF CANADA ON THE WORLD SCENE

Large questions surround the intertwining of culture and foreign policy: should the state concentrate on image building abroad, simply using culture to enhance the national image in a general way? Or should culture be enlisted as a servant of specific political, economic, and industrial goals? The arts community has been, and will continue to be, wary of being drawn into programs that are too goal specific, though the co-opting of culture may be compensated for by extraordinary opportunities for arts groups and individuals to broaden their horizons and experience the stimulation of contact with international audiences and artists.[16]

In this area there are some nagging problems for Canada. Our almost exclusive focus on Europe has been questioned and partially undermined, but opportunities to promote Canadian culture in Asia and the United States have yet to be consistently developed. The coordination of our cultural front abroad has been poor when compared with some similar operations, that of Australia, for example. Federal-provincial coordination has also been lacking, and some embarrassing conflicts have emerged.[17] The key factor here, of course, has been Quebec. The steady increase in Quebec nationalism means that this area will remain contentious; here separation would simplify things, and might actually stimulate a wide-ranging program of activities on the part of a reduced and Anglocentric Canadian culture. Conversely a surprising measure of cooperation between the parts of a divided Canada might even ensue, especially if – as I think likely – Quebec wakes up to find itself rather beleaguered by the dominant American cultural and linguistic machinery.

Current anglophone thinking on this matter is probably best represented by John Ralston Saul, who sees the export of Canadian culture as a key action in validating Canada's presence in the international scene in general.[18] He perhaps overrates the extent to which we exploit the American market, which he considers somewhat impenetrable and probably worth less in the long run than some others, but he advocates, as many do, the breaking of Canada's Eurocentric fixation in exporting our culture. He notes that Serge Joyal's investigations of some of these issues, carried out for the Department of Foreign Affairs, indicate a preference for setting up Canadian cultural centres around the world, somewhat on the model of the British Council (a separate cultural arm, such as the United States Information Service, was proposed by Applebaum-Hébert but never put into effect).[19]

While Saul suggests that coordination of cultural foreign policy be achieved through an instrument such as a "Cultural Foreign Strategies Committee" (which would include Foreign Affairs, Heritage, and Industry Canada representatives), I believe the solution lies in a Ministry of Culture liaising with Foreign Affairs.[20] Yet Saul is quite correct in thinking that one of the keys to the healthy development of Canadian culture lies in the export of Canadian creations. This will also serve the chief goals of Canadian foreign policy, which will have to deal not only with the perennial economic and political issues but also with new technology, with future developments in communications and information exchange, in short, with major social and cultural challenges, which seem likely to succeed the security/military challenges of the recent past.

Canada's cultural visibility around the world must increase, but this must be accompanied by change at home, by a rethinking of all our cultural structures and alignments. In this chapter I have attempted to spur creative thinking by suggesting some forms that such necessary changes might well take.

8 But Where's the Money to Come From?

*Is not a Patron, my lord, one who looks with unconcern on a man
struggling for life in the water, and when he has reached ground,
encumbers him with help?*
   – Samuel Johnson, Letter to Lord Chesterfield

M OST READERS WILL RECALL the ironic declaration of T. S.
Eliot who, in a mood of 1920s desolation, suggested that the
world would end "not with a bang but a whimper." The great
jazz musician Paul Desmond once saw a beautiful woman he fancied in
a nightclub accompanied by a rich old banker. Obviously a fan of Eliot's
poetry, Desmond quipped: "This is the way the world ends.... Not with
a whim, but a banker."

Desmond's sadder but wiser wit seems nicely to sum up the state of
the arts in Canada in the nineties. Artists and arts promoters look on
helplessly while the bankers seem to be busy taking over the realms of
beauty, introducing the uncomfortable issues of budgetary responsibility, profit and loss, and five-year development plans. The largess that
seemed almost boundless 20 years ago is no more. Those of us who
believe that the state should support the arts (and with funding, too) are
put to the test to answer the question: Where is the money to come
from?

Before I tackle that question, however, let me provide a little perspective on the question of arts development and financing in general.
Canada is hardly alone among the developed Western nations in facing
major funding problems for its arts industries. After the Second World
War, there was a significant increase of government support for the arts
in nearly all of the developed countries.[1] This support can be seen as part
of a general move toward "reconstruction." The war broke many cultural connections, constituting – apart from more fundamental woes – a

culture shock for many European and Asian countries, whose treasured traditions and artifacts were threatened, destroyed, or appropriated as part of the opportunism of the nations in conflict. The war had generated nationalist feelings; these, combined with an urgent desire to return to integrative pursuits after chaos (especially in Europe), furthered the growth of arts and culture.[2] We have seen that the Canadian expansionist rationale was nationalistic; in the United States it was humanistic, but also opportunistic: the National Endowment for the Arts was created (partially thanks to the Francophile Jacqueline Kennedy) and expanded – in the belief that it made political sense – from a budget of a few million to hundreds of million a mere decade later.[3]

In the postwar period the traditional state support for certain favoured arts institutions was expanded to include a vast array of new programs, clients, and forms of artistic activity. By the eighties these included "new forms of artistic expression, such as film, video, performance art, community art, and interdisciplinary art," and the traditionally unsupported activity of creating literature.[4]

During this period, great amounts were spent on building new facilities or on improving old ones, while arts activities in training schools, universities, and conservatories greatly increased. A strong international side emerged; hitherto isolated or unregarded social groups entered the arts picture. Significantly there was no cutting back on the older traditions of support; the expansionist mood was pervasive.

By the eighties and well into the nineties, the mood had changed. Cutbacks – or at best, zero growth – were in evidence everywhere, in line with the general international theme of financial responsibility, debt control, and the withdrawal of governments from providing "nonessential" services.

In Canada federal support of the arts continued to increase through the late eighties, but not in proportion to the demands put upon it by the artistic community (applications to the Canada Council rose by 32 percent during the decade), and not in relation to the increase in cost of living, or compared with the expense of producing art.[5] While the federal government's commitment to defence reached the $12 billion mark in 1992-93, and stood at the $10 billion level for employment and immigration, culture received about $2.9 billion (half of this for the CBC).[6] Because significant audience expansion had not been achieved, and provincial and municipal funding, after a huge postwar expansion, had levelled off or declined (much of this spending in any case was for libraries and heritage projects), the combined allocation of the three levels of government in recent years has amounted to about $15 a year for each Canadian. Canada's total government expenditure for culture, which remains at about 0.4 or 0.5 percent, seems inadequate in view of the magic number of 1 percent of total national expenditure that we see in France and Sweden. In 1991 Canadian corporations donated $70 million to the arts, which represented about 10 percent of total arts budgets.[7]

The classic philosophy of Canadian arts funding (which I alluded to in chapters 1 and 7) suggests that we have chosen a middle way between the European model of strong government support and the American way of strong private support. Certainly, in many respects, we compare rather unfavourably with the two other sectors of the suggested "triad." While Canada provides only 47 percent of the support for major non-profit performing-arts institutions, the United Kingdom and France contribute 70 and 80 percent respectively; in the United States, 58 percent of these costs is covered by subsidies and tax incentives.[8] In the first half of the nineties, this situation translated into constant alarms signalling the "imminent" collapse, or vulnerable condition, of one or another of Canada's major cultural agencies or producers (see chapter 6).

In retrospect it seems clear that Canada's arts community (like our other social interest groups) had been (during the past few decades) sleep-walking through a dream of limitless expansion, or at least avoiding fundamental issues that should have been addressed. Some would argue, plausibly, that it is difficult enough to make art, never mind to achieve a useful perspective on what you are doing. Whatever the case, the shortfalls, the cutbacks, the retrenchments, the closures have come as a dose of reality that may actually be sanguine. Certainly key issues have had to be addressed, as never before. What use are the arts to society? Is public funding a good thing? How can we expand audiences for the fine arts? Is it necessary to restructure our arts administration to meet the new challenges?

I will concentrate first on general funding policy. The recent financial crisis in the arts seems to have strengthened the case of those who believe that the state should not be involved in cultural funding at all. They see the situation as one of subsidizing unprofitable industries, or as a needless payment for what people are inclined to do by nature. If, as seems to be the case, art is a universal product of human creativity, why is it necessary to promote it by subsidies? Why invite state control of this "free human activity"? Why produce art that people don't want to buy? Why set up in judgement of artists and force them to have their art approved by committees? Such arguments range from the blatantly laissez-faire (and culturally crass) position of theorists such as Steven Globerman to the softer, more culturally sensitive position of "rejectionists" such as Andrew Coyne and John Metcalf.[9]

I will pass over the extreme laissez-faire doctrines, which I have sufficiently dealt with in my introduction. But what about the others? In a recent C B C discussion with Robert Fulford and Robert Enright, Coyne wondered

> why we . . . make Peter pay for Paul's creation or consumption of art when: a) Peter may not like Paul's taste in art; b) Paul may well be richer than Peter; c) Peter gets no benefit from Paul's consumption or creation of art; d) Paul could perfectly well pay for it himself; e) there may be more pressing uses for Peter's tax dollars.[10]

These objections may sound reasonable, but I believe that when you examine them they lose their force. I will take them one by one. First, we pay for many things in society that we do not personally approve. Recently the street on which I live was remodelled and resurfaced. I attended a meeting at which the plans were approved by a majority of my neighbours, but I did not particularly like these plans. My taxes helped to pay for the work, however, and I don't consider the result unreasonable. (I realize that I am no expert on road construction.) We cannot expect everyone in society to love paying taxes for the arts (or anything else). Yet so long as our parliamentary representatives vote for allotments on behalf of the arts, we can say they are doing the will of the country. Only a small minority of Canadians want to do away with such disbursements altogether, and very few would feel that their tax contribution turns them into arts specialists with the expertise to judge every product. In short, Peter's objection to certain kinds of art doesn't give him the right to withhold his taxes, any more than my taste in roadwork gave me the right to withhold mine.

Referring to Coyne's second point — that Paul is richer than Peter and should therefore pay for the art himself — I would suggest that, in terms of fundamentals, we are all part of this society. Opting out is not a privilege. If the arts are a fundamental part of civilization, as the best minds have judged, then we must support them or risk barbarism. Building more of an audience of Pauls — who have the money and want the product — is fine, but it doesn't constitute an argument for dispensing with Peter's (or my) tax contribution.

As to the third point, that the general benefits of the arts are nebulous, my answer is just take them away and see what kind of society we have. In two recent films, *Strawberry and Chocolate* (Cuban) and *Burnt by the Sun* (Russian), we see good people who preserve soul through culture, standing apart from the injustice and brutality of the Marxist ideology by connecting with the best of their own traditions. Their treasuring of "quality" embraces even the tiniest and seemingly most fragile artifacts: photographs, recordings, chairs, teacups. Modern society lacks strong religious faith, and in times of persecution, or when the state becomes rigid and brutal, what carries the power of soul is precisely what we pampered North Americans take for granted: the arts and culture.

Even as I write this, someone in my city is practising a Bach fugue or looking closely at a Rembrandt painting – and even on that level, the arts mean something to me. That person is spending time at an endeavour harmful to no one, one that creates a positive resonance in our society, and though the performance, the experience, remains solitary, I know that it connects my society with a society of the past in a meaningful way.

Coyne's third point, that Paul could perfectly well pay for it himself, still hangs on the notion that the arts are not a general social good. The overwhelming evidence is that they are.

As for the notion that there are better things to do with our tax dollars than to spend them on art, I consider this a red herring of an egregious sort. As if the money we hold back from the arts would be used to feed the starving, or to build better day-care centres! Let's be realistic: it would simply go to pay off government consultants, to fund "make-work" projects in someone's home riding, to increase defence spending, to subsidize foreign corporations, or to increase the travel allowances of the federal cabinet.

Coyne professes not to know what the arts are good for; I suggest that he turn to the master thinkers of our history; I suggest that he try to recall a civilization that we remember for something *other than* its arts and culture. No doubt the gross national product of the Sumerian economy, or the rate of water flow through the Roman sewers, or the wheat subsidies in fifth-century Athens are subjects that appeal to specialists, but when we think of those cultures, or of almost any past culture, what we tend to remember are the artistic achievements: in the cases I refer to, we think of the great *Epic of Gilgamesh,* of the poems of Virgil and Horace, of the Roman roads and aqueducts, of the Greek plays, or of the Parthenon. Even the great figures, the Alexanders, the Caesars, the Napoleons, lodge in our memories mostly thanks to literary and artistic sources, while the ordinary persons of the past may spring to life in a portrait, a sculpture, the fragment of a letter, or the graffiti of forgotten hands. Among other things, art is the concrete memory of humanity.

But the key argument against Coyne and others like him is that what they advocate (no matter how sincere their convictions) would – in Canada at least – throw art, quite naked, into the marketplace. Because we have no substantial structure of private support for art in Canada, every organization in the country would have to close down or cut back sharply. Ticket prices would skyrocket, because in many cases state subsidies serve to keep them under control.[11] The old idea of a democratic culture (I'm not talking about collectivist newspeak about "interest groups"), the idea that everyone should have the right to get acquainted with the best, would be lost. We would transform art into an elitist pursuit hardly seen even in the most blatant oligarchies of the past. Our society would be hopelessly divided. Most of our citizens would stand at the mercy of the American entertainment culture. If our government refused to support our arts, it would simply be derelict in its primary duty of protecting and preserving Canada as an integral culture (see chapter 4).

All of this is true, yet the fair-minded observer must admit that those who wish to retain and even bolster the present system of support for the arts and culture in this country seem to be whistling in the dark. It is clear that funds are limited, that audiences are limited, that our educational system, traditions, and way of life have failed to encourage an enthusiasm for the arts that is strong and widespread enough to sanction massive state funding. If this is the case, then aren't cutbacks in cultural funding inevitable? But can we not restructure in order to achieve more with less? To begin with, can we not *target our priorities* to achieve the goals we see as most central?

I have already suggested (in the previous chapter) a set of fundamental, though general, objectives for any coherent Canadian arts policy. In order to make clear how my restructuring would work, however, it is necessary to identify the more concrete and specific priorities that such a system would have in view; in other words what are the essential things that such a restructuring should accomplish for our arts and culture? In my view these priorities should be as follows.

1. To guarantee the survival of our major arts and cultural institutions.
2. To develop and sustain a public broadcasting system (CBC) that includes both an ad-free FM-stereo cultural radio network and an ad-free alternative television channel that would program Canadian culture.
3. To sustain a Canadian film industry.
4. To encourage cultural development through "start-up" or seed grants at the grass roots.
5. To reward cultural achievement by honouring artists who make outstanding contributions to our national culture.

Before I discuss what I consider to be the superfluous aspects of the present system, let me elaborate each of these points. First, our chief cultural institutions must be assured of survival. I refer to our great national and provincial galleries and museums, our symphony orchestras, our dance and opera companies and theatres, as well as some of the major festivals in the various regions. All of these institutions would be funded based on their cultural centrality, their importance to the audience they serve, and their past performance. The funding would include operating expenses and building funds where justified, and would be federal, provincial, and municipal – but some of it would hinge on rational plans for private-sector involvement, audience building, and other factors. Under this proposal the total amount of funding allotted for the support of institutions would decrease from the present level, because the criteria that would have to be met would exclude many arts groups now receiving grants.

Second, it seems obvious to me that we can have no cultural sovereignty unless we have a healthy national public broadcasting system, one that is mandated to present the best of Canadian and world culture on both radio and TV.

Third, we also need a strong basis for the funding of feature films, along the lines of the present Telefilm Canada.

Fourth, there can be little health in a system that does not give some incentive to new artists and organizations. These grants would only include initial funding, however. Once launched, both individual artists and organizations would have to develop their own survival plans.

Fifth, we should always have in place a system of honours and prizes for artists who have endured and who represent the best of the Canadian spirit in each generation. The Governor General's Awards, the Molson Prize, the Giller Prize, and the myriad other prizes and contests that exist should be made widely known to the public. New prizes and contests should be created, and "chairs" for artists should be established in our universities – all to be funded wherever possible by the private sector, but with overall coordination (and especially promotion) by the Ministry of Culture.

The above plan should be accompanied by a shift in the way we finance the arts. Government outlays that must continually increase are not to be thought of; what is needed are incentive-type measures that encourage private-sector contributions to the arts.

The aim, of course, should not be to *replace* public funding – this is a naive goal; furthermore, the American example shows that private-sector funding tends to increase when the level of public funding is high. The key to improving contributions lies in tax advantages. "Almost every study directed at business support for the arts has confirmed that tax advantages are the one thing government can hold out which will have an effect."[12] However, it is no simple matter to create tax structures that encourage support of the arts, as we can see from the American example, where over the decades the scope and nature of private and corporate giving have been closely linked to changes in the tax system. Only in the past two decades, and thanks to the existence of the Council for Business and the Arts in Canada, has art really found a place on the corporate agenda here.[13] The Arnold Edinborough business forums, which help to link the arts to business in smaller Canadian communities, constitute another positive sign. But what is needed now is a complete reexamination of the arts-business connection at the highest levels, with a view to creating a tax structure that would double or triple private-sector contributions to the arts. The pressure for such restructuring, however, can only come from artists, and this would seem to constitute the most promising central goal for arts lobbies during the next several years.

Artists should also be lobbying for a change proposed in the eighties by George Woodcock and others: namely, that "the cost of tickets to performing art shows and of Canadian books and recordings should be regarded as tax deductible."[14] This concession would mean raising the individual limit for charitable donations, or creating a special category for arts support, and allowing a multiple of the ticket price to be deductible. The removal of the GST (and where applicable) the PST on books would be enormously helpful.

There should be a national lottery for the arts. It could be called "The Mona Lisa Lottery," with the Western world's most famous icon stamped on the tickets (or perhaps "The Jack Pine Lottery," if we wish a Canadian association); in any case, it would be advertised with catchy slogans – for example, "Will the Mona Lisa Smile on You?" The lottery must be run with panache; Canadian puritanism about these things must be swept aside. (The Wintario Challenge Grant Program in Ontario in 1980-83 used lottery revenues to fund 34 major arts organizations.)[15] The argument that we already have too many lotteries is countered by the fact that here would be a lottery that every arts lover in Canada could support with enthusiasm and a sense of doing good things for the cause. It would have the advantage of drawing cash support for the arts from those who actually use the arts resources. And there are precedents: New Zealand, Ireland, and Finland use lotteries with great success in financing the arts.

Other innovations in arts funding must be explored in Canada. Among the most promising are the following.[16]

1. Contractual agreements between government funders and arts organizations receiving the grants. These contracts specify the goals of the funding and enable governments to monitor results and relate the grants to community objectives.

2. Matching or incentive grants. In the United States, where this

approach is a major part of arts funding, it has been possible to set goals that frame the uses of the money disbursed, thus connecting funding with overall policy objectives. The most recent American programs aim at achieving excellence in the arts, creating access to the arts, improving appreciation of the arts, and strengthening support systems for the arts. Because the matching-grant ratio is $3 for every government dollar invested, this approach automatically generates money from the private sector. Variations of this kind of program, aimed at increasing corporate sponsorship, are now in effect in Great Britain and France, with generally positive results.

3. Stabilization funds should be generated for large arts organizations so that they can build capital reserves and reduce the pressures leading to cash-flow crises. (We can see how badly needed these funds are in view of what many arts organizations in Canada have gone through in the nineties.) Such funds must come from private sources (such as foundations) and be carefully administered and monitored.

The shifts in funding strategies are designed to correlate with the overall cultural goals I outlined above. The most striking departure from tradition in all this is perhaps my suggestion that almost all funding of individual artists be eliminated. Let me make myself clear. I believe that all *direct* grants to individuals, except in the case of some new creative artists, should be eliminated. Grants to writers should be largely abolished. Writers should be paid through the public-lending-right mechanism. Some grants could be available on a onetime basis to subsidize a deserving writer's first work, but thereafter he or she should have to deal with the marketplace.

While the saving from ceasing to give individual-artist grants would not be enormous (they comprise approximately 10 to 15 percent of Canada Council grants), I believe it is time to take the step of abolishing them.[17] My reasons are straightforward. In times of crisis the least necessary expenditures must go. Does anyone doubt that these are the least necessary? Another point: it is impossible to distribute individual grant money fairly. The Council peer-evaluation system simply doesn't work. I have served on enough Canada Council juries to be aware of the flaws of the system. Many jurors are honest and diligent, but one can only agree with John Metcalf that "some do arrive with not-deeply-hidden agendas."[18] Because the Council does not even use a "blind jury" system (many other granting agencies do), one sees cronyism, the savaging of some applications by jury members hostile to the applicants and, recently, an egregious bending of the rules in favour of applicants from supposedly "disadvantaged" groups. In practice "peer review" is simply neither broad nor objective enough. I don't believe writers should get grants at all, except for initial small subsidies to confirm that they have produced some good work and have reasonable expectations of producing more. (Helpful criticism in the past sometimes came with rejections from editors and publishers, but this was never common, and under the present commercialized system, it is impossible to expect such feedback. These "start-up" grants would fill the void.)

In the case of initial literary grants, however, I would use blind juries, and would not use juries composed only of professional writers. I would use writers, ordinary citizens who are good readers, disinterested publishers, and others – and I am confident that under such a system, the results would be much better.

In any case, writers have traditionally *not* been state-subsidized; the notion that they *should be* is part of the postwar cultural boom, and it appears to be mistaken. Because I have already suggested that Canada Council funding was an important part of the flowering of postwar Canadian culture, my position here may seem self-contradictory. It is not. In the case of literature, seed money was right and proper and did the job of getting Canadians into the writing game, while also providing them with presses that might publish their work; partially because of this activity an audience sprang up from almost nowhere. The system did its job, I believe, but that is no reason for it to continue indefinitely. Both Woodcock and Metcalf emphasize the traditional necessity for a writer to learn the craft through trial and error, to improve his or her work to the point where it can be enjoyed by a reasonable number of readers, including educated and knowledgeable peers; this approach is not encouraged by the present system. At the house of a book reviewer and columnist for one of our major newspapers I recall the sight of a table full of the "latest Canadian small press books." It was not an encouraging sight. It is well-known that once on the gravy train writers can go on getting grants down the road, even when their initial creative powers, if any, have waned. This is a wasted resource as far as our cultural needs go.

I would give no grants at all to small presses. The past few decades of state intervention have helped to create a diverse and eager readership for Canadian books. (Not, however, including people such as the notorious Chuck Cook, former Tory MP from North Vancouver, whose motto was "Not too much Canadian stuff . . . it's just not good enough.")[19] Computer technology has made production easier, and there is no reason to fund multiple copies of fiction or poetry that the small presses have no idea how to market (often because no one wants to read it).

Literary presses should be challenged now to work toward profitability; they should support what they believe in, learn how to do marketing, and stop filling the shelves with dutiful and pointless material, paid for at the taxpayers' expense. John Ralston Saul has proposed a single distribution agency for Canadian books, one that would be enormously useful in penetrating the international market. Such an agency, which would require only partial funding from government, would expand the market for Canadian writers in a way that direct subsidies to publishers can never do.

Canadian films are up against much tougher odds. The creation of a Ministry of Mass Communications would enable us to give the film industry the sensitive attention it needs to hold its own against the American industry. The film industry should be subsidized through taxes paid by exhibitors at the box office; quotas for Canadian films would bring the market share to a reasonable minimum, say, 10 percent, distributed through a central Canadian agency. Contrast this approach with some of the pathetic schemes of the past, such as giving Americans an unrestricted market here in exchange for some favourable mention of Canada in American films.[20]

The results of all these changes would be striking. The federal government would at last have chosen a protectionist policy for the arts that would guarantee the survival of our culture, without taking on burdens that are financially unreasonable and possibly self-defeating. The more absurd forms of subsidy would be eliminated. The major channels of cultural communication would be kept open: our great national institutions, our important regional centres and companies, would survive. Television, radio, and films, key elements in any national cultural strategy, would also be secured. New arts organizations – small galleries, collectives, dance groups, and so on – could count on federal or provincial funding only on a start-up basis. There would be no public subsidies after the initial grant, and even those grants would be available only to groups offering plans of high artistic merit, with some kind of down-the-road survival possibility. If new organizations succeed in establishing themselves, they could become part of the essential core of our cultural life, going to the private sector for further support under one of the funding schemes detailed above, but individual artists, after start-up, would *in no case* be subsidized.

What about the selection process, the channelling of funds, how would this be improved? Would we not end up with a centralized system without much flexibility? Would we not be preserving the fossils and sacrificing the new and vital groups, the avant-garde?

I don't believe that it would be difficult to compile a list of the major arts organizations across the country, to pinpoint those institutions whose survival is essential to the cultural life of Canada – or to add to the list when new organizations prove their quality. None of these decisions should be purely bureaucratic, either: a broad base of informed members of the community should be engaged in the process of choosing and monitoring these key organizations. Many of our citizens who go to concerts or visit galleries, those who are interested in, and basically knowledgeable about, the arts, should share with the experts and bureaucrats the task of preserving the cultural heritage of this country.

Here, as elsewhere, the role of a Ministry of Culture should be to encourage as much local participation as possible, and provincial and municipal involvement in any new cultural network would be major (increasing even from the present levels), while new partnerships with the private sector should be fostered by all levels of government. As I pointed out in the previous chapter, in the United States the National Endowment for the Arts funnels much of its funding to local (state) arts agencies; there is no reason to maintain the bureaucratic centrality of the Canada Council here.[21]

Under the system I propose a healthy share of federal funding would be channelled to provincial, and ultimately to municipal, agencies. Promising new groups could be targeted locally and initially funded; some would be experimental, but we would free ourselves from the absurdity of the steady and guaranteed funding of "far-out" art – which, by its very nature, should be free of state support. Experimental art surely ought to remain marginal, if it is not actually underground, and should never become part of a state-subsidized system. This is not to suggest that a national Art Bank could not select experimental pieces, for example, or that a nationally supported theatre, dance, or opera company could not take artistic risks, but only that groups and organizations that produced only marginal or far-out material would not be state-supported. They would be helped by the state in many ways (on the promotional and communications sides, for example), but they would not be "pets" of the state, a situation that could only decrease their potency, and that would seem to be self-defeating as far as their artistic aims are concerned. A state-subsidized avant-garde is an absurdity.

If we eliminate grants to all but an essential core of cultural producers, if we virtually eliminate all individual arts grants, if we draw the public into the selection and monitoring process and root our artistic organizations in the community, while giving them a national profile and a new potency of coast-to-coast communication and exchange, then we will go forward with confidence as a culture and a nation into the next century.

If every one of my proposals were put into effect, if the relevant government ministries were reorganized, if funding were redistributed as I suggest, if local initiatives and new connections with the business community were established, and the tax reforms I have suggested were put into effect, then the whole situation for culture in this country would stabilize. Arts organizations would no longer have to beg for crisis funding; governments would be able to set goals and control spending; the private sector would be drawn into arts funding in a more consistent way. We need courage and determination at all levels to make these changes, but what is the alternative? If the federal government refuses to reorganize its cultural apparatus, and there is no redistribution of funding, then we face the worst kind of "market" chaos, that is, what survives may have nothing to do with coherent national objectives: Canadian culture, as such, will disappear. And I am not alluding to the disappearance of a few avant-garde galleries, or a few marginal writers; I'm envisaging a country that has allowed its grass-roots creativity to perish, a country that will allow itself to be conned by Disneyland, Madonna, and Oprah's daily lineup of bleeding hearts. Paul Bernardo was bad enough, but anyone who reads Neil Postman with acuity will realize that if we capitulate to the American cultural machinery, then O. J. Simpson cannot be far behind.

In all of this, the audience remains of key importance. Many organizations have found creative solutions to the apparent levelling off or decline of interest in the arts and culture in this country, but there remains much alarm and some confusion. In the next chapter I make suggestions for a new educational approach that I believe would begin to create a solid future for the arts in Canada. The idea of a national campaign along the lines of PARTICIPACTION is certainly a good one.[22] But there are other necessities. The fracturing of audiences into interest groups has to be reversed. There are too many events pushed on the public by ideologically tuned artists who have forgotten the universal element in art. I recently heard a playwright explaining her play in a way that reduced the whole exercise (and, alas, it *sounded* like an exercise) to a sociological position; we heard a lot about "the problem of communication" and "excluded or marginalized peoples," but nothing about ordinary human emotion – nothing about love or hate; nothing about dramatic power, clashes, conflicts; nothing about pathos and yearning, or beauty and sadness and joy. Composers are beginning to realize that no one is interested in their relation to the second Viennese school, or to aleatory methods, or to the Third World, or to the Amazon ecology. What we want is beautiful and powerful music – which we are beginning to get again. Playwrights, poets, and novelists take note: audiences are fed up with your self-indulgences. No government is going to put out our tax money in the name of Canadian content if you are not capable of delivering something of emotional power, something that unites us in pleasure (which may be painful and shocking, too!) rather than dividing us on the basis of ideas.

Massey and his associates were right; in the fifties it was historically necessary for the Canadian government to intervene with financial support in order to preserve and encourage Canadian culture. But the intervention was not uniformly successful, not because there was too little funding, but because some of the policies were badly conceived or misguided, or they overlooked necessities such as education, building an audience for culture, and enlisting more support from the private sector. Certain things were botched, notably the evolution of CBC Television. Later (perhaps inevitably) politics became a factor; the Canada Council enlisted the concept of a national culture against Quebec separatists – perhaps a good thing – and – certainly a bad thing – political correctness was officially sanctioned and supported.

What I propose here is a change of emphasis. We must give a new visibility to the arts through a Ministry of Culture, and place communications (and the mass-media arts) in a separate ministry. The role of the Canada Council should be modified in order to protect our essential arts institutions; publishing and writers should be supported in ways that do not encourage productivity for its own sake. We should have strong public broadcasting, both in radio and television. A national arts communication network should be set up, and a system of culture houses spanning the country established, using present facilities. Business should be further encouraged to support the arts, and a national arts lottery should be established.

If all these changes were put into effect, they would end the expectation of blanket government funding of all "worthy" arts activities, yet provide stable funding for our major institutions and a sufficiently broad program of incentives for new work. The arts budget would be increased, thanks to lottery funds, tax incentives, and increased participation of the public, which would come about due to an improvement in the sphere of promotion and communications. Our arts would be strongly rooted in the community, yet would have a powerful national profile. All of which would go a long way toward taking our culture on a creative path into the next century.

9 The Arts and Education

Fine art is that in which the hand, the head and the heart of man go together.
— John Ruskin, *The Two Paths*

HOW AND WHY should education promote the arts and culture? What forms should this promotion take? In an extensive report jointly commissioned by the Canada Council and the Social Sciences and Humanities Research Council of Canada, a team of scholars from the University of Victoria and the University of British Columbia examined the question of arts literacy in Canada. The results appeared in a document entitled *The State of the Art,* which is lively and useful, isolates some of the basic problems for contemporary Canadian culture, and identifies and summarizes various opinions on how to deal with these problems. Unfortunately, though the authors conclude by offering 22 recommendations for action, *every one of them is a research proposal.*[1] This, I suppose, is par for the course for a team of professors.

More helpfully the Victoria Colloquium on Arts Literacy (held in 1992 as part of the preparation for the book mentioned) agreed on a few characteristics of the person who is literate in the arts.[2] Such a person

- seeks out art experiences
- perceives and responds to the qualities of the work
- is knowledgeable about the specific codes of arts forms (tradition, history, canon, vocabulary)
- has experience with the creative process of the arts, and exercises discernment (makes informed choices) in selecting arts experiences.

I will deal with two aspects of arts education that take for granted (and pretty well incorporate) the above four points. I ask myself the question: what should students learn about the arts? My approach is straightforward, though not simple in implication or consequence. Ultimately I am concerned with the learning process, whereas the four points simply state overall goals.

First, students must acquire *knowledge* of the great traditions of art, a knowledge sadly lacking in our population; in this area the schools of the recent past have almost completely failed us. *Participation* in the arts by young people is another key goal, and here the schools have done a much better job.

As far as conveying knowledge of the arts is concerned, there are certain ironies in our situation that should be noted. First, while parents and educators from time to time get exercised about the failure of our schools to teach such things as science and mathematics, they rarely complain about the corresponding failure to teach the arts. This is because they themselves have no sense of the value of the arts and culture, because they regard this area of human knowledge as secondary, passé, nonfunctional, as mere entertainment, unprofitable in terms of job prospects (unless you are going to be a TV star), and sometimes as downright dangerous and threatening.

Part of the reason why arts and culture, as a subject of study, have made little headway in our schools is that North Americans have largely given up the study of history. It is possible to go through the primary and secondary Canadian education system in the best institutions and to learn almost no history, to have no sense of how Canada stands in relation to its own traditions and to the traditions that created it. This has not always been so in North America. I was taught an outline of Greek history in grade 4; in high school we had to write exams on the French Revolution and Bismarck. Today the little that is taught is often structural material on "government," rather than a thoroughgoing investigation of the main figures and forces in world history, without which it is difficult to imagine any cultural study worth its name being undertaken. "Hey! I like Bach! He's cool!" is no substitute for knowing that Bach is a figure of the Baroque and composed as he did, for whom he did, and with the inspiration he did for understandable (though not predetermined) historical reasons.

It is particularly surprising, now that school boards have policies about the dangers of Eurocentrism and are busy (quite rightly) inculcating tolerance for immigrant cultures, that our students have no knowledge of European culture.[3] I would hazard a guess that any student seriously afflicted with Eurocentrism would fill a good teacher with delight; just to have a young person actually know where Europe is, what cultures it has encompassed, and to have a real feel for them, would be an achievement that would have most teachers turning handsprings.

Teachers tell me that the problem they face teaching the arts as a subject, putting young people in touch with the creative past, whether in music, literature, or art history, is that it tends to create "just one more subject," one requiring all the standard and seemingly boring skills of memorization, quizzes, and exams. This material, they say, seems difficult of access for many young Canadians; it turns the arts into a "discipline" rather than a pleasure.

What a pity! It would be much easier if there were a simple brain implant, a memory elixir, a computer program that would do all the work! Let's face it, learning occasionally does require memorization, study, and discipline. If students can handle verb conjugations and noun endings in foreign languages, if they can memorize the complex terms of ecological study or deal with math formulas, then schemas of art or music history should not terrify them.

Yet I must emphasize my firm conviction that *there is no effective arts education unless the learner is committed, enthusiastic, and willing to learn and even participate.* If one wants to be literate in music history, one must know something at least about Bach, but if the experience of Bach arouses no enthusiasm in the student, then − if the teaching is to be effective − another entry point must be sought.

Good programs and bold teachers, without spoon-feeding, or dropping the class to the "arts-identikit" level, can do much to improve the background knowledge of students. One imaginative grade 3 teacher in Ottawa, for example, successfully introduced her students to art history (almost certainly because she conveyed her own enthusiasm and the sense that what she was talking about was important).[4] She began by simply bringing to class illustrated material on Picasso. She talked about the life of the painter (interestingly the children loved this approach); then using postcards, reproductions, appealing books, and so on, she introduced the era in which Picasso worked, and explained the various techniques and something about the style of his work. The students were then set to work making their own improvisations after the pieces they most admired. Their enthusiasm was so great that they demanded that more painters be introduced, and this occurred. A trip to the National Gallery of Canada followed, with some hands-on activities. In Birmingham, Alabama, a similar (though privately financed) program introduced a number of ghetto children to the life and work of Josiah Wedgwood, the English pottery maker. The study included a detailed examination of his life and demonstrated how the pottery was produced; then the children produced their own pottery, using motifs significant to them.[5]

I suspect that many of the children who go through programs such as this (I went through a similar one myself in grade school, and they are common in Europe) grow up with an enthusiastic interest in art and its production, and parallel activities in the case of music and literature would no doubt have similar results. Experience also suggests that the best way to teach the history of the arts at all levels is to indicate the *process* nature of the arts. We should emphasize how past and present mingle in the *historical* process in which art unfolds, how the grasp of one aspect of art leads us to understand another in quite a different sphere, how artists and audiences interact, how one's own perceptions shift and change as one acquires knowledge and experience. It is, of course, also extremely useful to incorporate some degree of performance or demonstration in any course designed to promote arts literacy. And there are ways of putting process and practice together that can inspire creative learning even in resistant students.

One of the most ingenious principles of current grade-school education is that of an "integrated thematic curriculum," which refers to breaking down category boundaries and understanding a subject not in isolation but in terms of its place in a process. Instead of teaching about the habits of owls, you choose the category "night" and construct a lesson involving a whole set of related phenomena that have to do with the experience of night, one of which might be owls. Thus, the owl is understood in context rather than in isolation. This is the opposite of Mr. Gradgrind's teaching about the horse in Dickens's *Hard Times,* in which the horse is defined so as to exclude everything that is contextual to it, and made unreal as a result.

In grade schools it would be quite possible to focus on some arts object – such as the drum – with wide ramifications. Children love drums and are at home with them; at the same time, the drum has huge cross-cultural significance: as a primitive signal; as a ritual instrument sending the shaman to the other world; in a military band; as a subtle or aggressive note of black liberation in jazz; in Haydn's Drum Roll Symphony; in the sound of the side drum in Nielsen's Fifth Symphony, beating its courageous (or manic) defiance against the overbearing orchestra. Some drum virtuosi representing a few of these areas would be an essential adjunct to such a course. It would surely inspire and excite the children (though it might drive some teachers crazy unless used in moderation!). Here, though, is a way of getting into the heart of many cultures and many eras, a vehicle for carrying us from one level of culture to another, a way of providing an entrée to music that would not fail to teach all children something fundamental about music and culture. Nor need this thematic and presentational approach prevent the learning from being systematic and thorough, for the lessons and demonstrations could be accompanied by a fairly rigorous program of factual and historical information about cultures and eras, and about the technology and even the physics of music making.

While some might object that new programs to promote the arts in schools would require specially trained teachers, or large additional expenditures, this is surely not the case.[6] Most school boards have the expertise to mount such a program, teacher exchanges can be arranged, and arts organizations in many cases can provide written guidelines and visiting artists. Useful arts curricula already exist across the country; it only requires a commitment on the provincial level to begin to provide coherent cultural education in our school systems.[7]

In all of these specifics I have carefully refrained from invoking the new technology; I have not suggested that students be loaded with CD-ROM programs taking them "inside" Beethoven's Fifth Symphony or Tolstoy's *War and Peace,* or that virtual reality should provide virtual walking tours of the Parthenon (though it probably will).

The current idolatry of the computer as an educational tool is intelligently exposed in Neil Postman's dissection of "technopoly."[8] The computer, hailed as the panacea for all educational ills, represents the mindless acceptance of the assumptions of a technological society, in which efficiency and stimulation are the chief values. Hardly a day goes by that we are not presented with some upbeat television feature story (and we know how accurate, how profound, they are!) in which we are shown students busily involved with some "revolutionary" software that is guaranteed to put them in touch with vast amounts of "useful" information. The ultimate purpose of this "getting in touch" is never mentioned, nor is the value of the information questioned. (Is it information we want, or the ability to think and feel from our own centres? Is there a difference between information and wisdom, between factual knowledge and connoisseurship?)

Mastering a computer is a technological, not a creative, achievement. It can be a useful skill, like driving a car, but driving skills do not necessarily make better or wiser citizens, and neither do computers. They are dependent upon software; software has boundaries and limitations. In a computer program everything is framed and known (despite the "limitless" possibilities of new displays and networking). It's more to the point to get students to integrate and develop unprogrammed knowledge that comes from many sources: listening to teachers and experts, reading, quiet thinking times, free exploration with camera or notebook, walks and conversations with friends, and observations of life. Such knowledge cannot be framed by a screen or acquired at a keyboard. One is told that the computer has unlimited possibilities; in fact, in terms of creativity, the human brain is the only limitless instrument our planet has produced.

As computers become ubiquitous, they tend to replace the person-to-person, "tacit" interaction that is the heart of the relationship between a teacher and a student. Despite their ability to do many tricks of referencing and combining, computers are a weak teaching vehicle compared with this face-to-face encounter. I once did a creativity workshop with a wise woman, an artist, named Edith Wallace. She used scissors, coloured paper, and paste with an effectiveness that would put any computer program I have seen to shame.

It is no accident that computers are being pushed into the classroom in record numbers. This push is certainly not the result of anyone's deep conviction about learning, or because the pedagogical goals require it. Like much else in our society, it results from a calculated marketing strategy, furthered by the unthinking idolatry of technology. The Canadian government, as well as private industry, is committed to developing computers and computer programs because they are part of the "new economy," profitable and chic; we now have many firms that need to sell their products, and large numbers of young people entering the computer industry every day.[9] It makes economic sense to hawk computer machinery to the school systems. (But does it make educational sense?) Yes, say the government think tanks, the new gurus rhapsodizing about the wonders in store for our society once interactive computers, virtual reality programs, telecomputers, and other technological vehicles are universal. Yet when one reads the fine print, some of the prognostications take on a different tone. We hear about addiction, loss of literacy, loss of control of information, closed loops, narcissism, new possibilities of Big Brotherism, and the triumph of the entertainment society. (Children still spend most of their computer time playing games.)

If the above seems an unduly suspicious analysis, consider the following fact. In this media-saturated society, why is it that we spend so little time teaching our children how to read the media? The most potent educational tool in our society is no longer the school; it is television. Yet students still go all the way to university before they are likely to be exposed to anything like a critical analysis of this medium, which is their central information and entertainment source. Northrop Frye, Neil Postman, in fact, a wide spectrum of commentators, have urged that such training be put in place, and from the earliest years.[10] It would be quite easy to design a curriculum that would help even young children deal with television, that would enable them to read the medium and to disengage somewhat from the messages constantly assaulting them. But it is unlikely that communications companies or private business would rush to fund such a curriculum, and many parents, unaware of the negative potential of their children's viewing habits, or themselves dependent on the small screen for a life focus, would no doubt disapprove of time spent in the classroom on this subject.

We don't need computers to teach the arts, though as an adjunct they may have their uses; we don't need TV, film, video, CDs, and tapes to instruct our students, though these media can serve a purpose if judiciously used. Items such as the Toronto-produced educational video *Beethoven Lives Upstairs* make some instruction programs easier to mount. But what we need above all are good teachers, artists willing to communicate their passions, and a curriculum enriched by the study of the arts.

At the university level, where one might expect imaginative courses in the arts, or a requirement that every student take at least one course in cultural history, the arts and culture are also badly served. Today a B.A. after a student's name tells us almost nothing about that student's grasp of cultural history. Most universities in Canada overflow with the technology and artifacts of popular culture; college radio stations play rock music almost exclusively; courses in art and music do not deal with aesthetics or historical issues, or they transform aesthetics and history into endless pseudo-sociological discussions of gender, race, and class – if they deal with the great works of Western art at all, it is likely in order to deconstruct them. Students learn a veritable dictionary of postmodern critical jargon that allows them to distance themselves immeasurably from anything like a strong personal involvement with the works in question; criticism becomes more important than experience of the artwork. This critical approach might be valuable if the students were coming to these courses after previous naive, enthusiastic encounters with the works analyzed. But this isn't the case. They may never have heard Bach in much depth or quantity; they may never have seen many Gauguins. They have simply not experienced enough art to form their own passionate likes and dislikes, to identify their own personal treasures which, after a while, they would learn how to explain and defend. They have not even been compelled to grasp important works in an objective context. As a result, they learn what to think before they know how to feel; they learn how to take a work apart (using a narrow ideological focus), but are baffled as to how to place it within the great tradition of Western culture (which, in any case, has been debunked for them in advance).

This kind of higher education, coming after the failure of the grade schools, has produced a generation of students who are almost com-

pletely indifferent to, and illiterate about, the arts. No wonder the attendance at cultural events and institutions has not risen, despite the increase
in the number of university graduates. No wonder there is so little real
support for the arts among the Canadian public. No wonder our society
considers aesthetic issues about as abstruse (though not quite so relevant)
as nuclear physics.

This basic failure of education (which afflicts the United States as
much as Canada) has given rise to books such as E. D. Hirsch, Jr.'s *Cultural
Literacy* and *The Cultural Literacy Encyclopedia,* which attempt to provide
the adult who is uneasy about his or her lack of knowledge with an
overview of culturally significant figures. But as Neil Postman's critique
of this endeavour makes clear, the enterprise is self-defeating in a culture
that equates celebrity with achievement; technology itself offers an
impossible glut of information, and we lack agreed-upon principles of
selection.[11]

No, the problem of cultural illiteracy must be solved much earlier;
reach-me-down guidebooks are not the answer, and in any case argue a
lack of involvement, an alienation from cultural activities on the part of
even the so-called well-educated person, that is alarming.

To address this problem in Canada, one must deal with complex
issues, chiefly because educational responsibilities lie with the provinces;
it would be much easier to design a program if there were a national
Ministry of Education which, as in France and other countries, would
assume part of the responsibility for promoting cultural literacy. Because
that option is probably not a likely one in the near future, I would point
to the possibility of Cultural Education Councils, which I have discussed
in chapter 7. They would initiate and disseminate new techniques of presenting the arts and culture in schools and universities, and because they
would be composed of artists and educators, as well as bureaucrats and
administrators, the process of putting ideas into existing systems would
be shortened. Through these councils meaningful issues could be isolated and dealt with; specific programs could be designed; the classroom
and the arts community could be brought together. Even symbolically
this would be a useful gesture, because it would confirm the importance
of the arts in education, but practically it might be a marvellous funnel
for experiments in teaching the arts at all levels, a clearinghouse of creative ideas. Such exchanges of information would help the schools to
make rational plans; the present system, which has some inspired elements, is also very hit and miss, and lacks a fundamental declaration of
purpose, despite such eloquent "mission statements" as that found in
Ontario's *The Common Curriculum,* to which I allude below.

Imaginative programs do exist at the university level (and if we had an arts and cultural-information network such as I describe, they would be better known across the country). At the University of Windsor in Ontario, for example, there is a course called "Culture and Ideas," which treats cultural history in chronological study units that include all the arts and some of the general culture of a given period.[12] In this program students are exposed to live performances, demonstrations, or tours that amplify the lecture material and help to make the arts a living reality, rather than a theoretical proposition. In teaching Romantic literature, I myself (long before the current fad for multimedia instruction) required that students produce scripts incorporating slides, appropriate music, and other material, all designed to embody some important theme of that cultural epoch. The important thing about this exercise is that the material was not preformulated; it required the students to undertake their own research and to produce imaginative (and accurate) narratives.

Recently I designed a program that I call "cultural mapping," the purpose of which is to introduce specific cultural traditions to university students, to fill the void in a student's background by highlighting, for some chosen era, a number of major figures in a variety of arts and cultural pursuits. The assumption here is that the students will be only vaguely acquainted with the artists or works in question, and do not need a highly charged or committed critical apparatus as much as they need to experience the material, to feel its expressive power, to understand the form of each work and its relation to its era, as well as its connection with the culture that preceded and followed it. The danger of a "gee whiz!" approach is offset by the requirement that the student master the material in various formal ways. This kind of integrated arts program is an absolute necessity in a society in which students remain untrained in aesthetic values and are so bombarded with the artifacts of popular culture. Universities must increasingly take on the task of introducing them to the serious culture that offers profundity and a critique of life that will serve them well as human beings and citizens later on.

Knowledge of the arts and cultural history should be part of the central curriculum of both our schools and universities. Students should be required to know something of the great works of the past, certainly the great works of the Judaic-Christian-European tradition. They should know Canadian traditions, past and present. How many high school students could identify a single member of the Group of Seven? How many have seen the work of Alex Colville or Jack Shadbolt? How many have heard a recording of Glenn Gould playing Bach, or the music of R. Murray Schafer or Harry Somers? How many have studied more than one Canadian novelist or poet in a high school course? The curriculum should also include, where possible, some acquaintance with the works of other cultures, especially those that form part of the Canadian mosaic. The goal should be to produce university and even high school graduates with a sense of the power of aesthetic culture, with some notion of the traditions of the past; it should provide them with a framework to understand what is happening in the present.

Arts history is one thing; arts practice is another. In many respects schools and universities are doing a far better job with the latter. If we look at a well-conceived guide document for schools such as Ontario's *The Common Curriculum* (1993), we find a strong endorsement of the value of both aspects of arts study.[13] This document (which applies specifically to grades 1 to 9) is representative of the most knowledgeable kind of arts-curriculum planning, though its philosophy and goals are hardly embedded in the Ontario curriculum, at either the grade school or the high school level.

The Common Curriculum speaks of the necessity of young students understanding form and "exploring meaning" in the arts. It suggests, quite rightly, that "the arts are closely interrelated and share many formal characteristics, such as pattern, texture, rhythm and overall structure." It asserts that "an understanding of form in one artistic discipline . . . is useful in understanding form in another." Other aesthetic aspects of the arts are proposed for study, and it is asserted that "works of art are influenced by and illuminate the political, economic, cultural and social milieu and the environmental conditions of the time when they were created."[14]

On the creative side, *The Common Curriculum* speaks out, though a bit tentatively and perhaps too optimistically, in favour of the student's creative involvement in the arts, suggesting that "as students become familiar with the tools, materials, processes, and techniques required to create their own works, they will develop a deeper understanding of the achievements of artists whose works they are studying."[15]

The rhetoric is beyond reproach, but how are these goals to be realized? In the primary schools, we have to rely on creative teachers such as the one I mentioned earlier, with her Picasso show. But though high school guidelines everywhere in Canada are based on similar assumptions, the problem at that level is more crucial and needs to be more coherently addressed by means of permanent programs. Ontario has no fewer than 30 "arts enrichment" high schools, and it is possible that a curriculum promoting at least some of the above, or equivalent, objectives could be managed in such a specialized context. But in the general high school, where would one find the time and the expertise to accomplish them?

To zero in on this question a little, let me suggest the following. First, students entering high school cannot be expected to have any idea of the history and power of the arts, because North American entertainment culture occupies most of their time since birth, to the exclusion of everything else. The schools therefore owe the student three things, which I will name in sequential order (though in any useful program, the three would have to overlap and be integrated): *experience, instruction,* and *participation.*

What gets novices excited about the arts is most often a striking experience of an artwork: a child is dragged by well-intentioned parents to the opera and finds it magical; a young man or woman walks into a gallery and sees a painting that becomes a lifetime treasure; a high school theatre trip results in an enduring enthusiasm. These are accidental occurrences, however; the problem for the school is that calculated ones often don't work.

One way to make them work would be to tie them to themes that are already correlated with the developmental patterns and age interests of the students. Themes such as "heroism," "love," and "evil" (there are many others) have a strong appeal to this (high school) age group. The school or an individual teacher could tip the scales in favour of a positive arts experience by lining up events around such key themes, without assuming that the structure is more important than the material studied.

Heroism could be explored through *Antony and Cleopatra* or *Mother Courage,* through Goya's etchings on the *Disasters of War,* through the Symphony Fantastique, a Mahler symphony, or a film such as *Paths of Glory.* Subtle variations on such a broad theme would occur to any intelligent teacher, and the choices could be correlated (as the above are not) with a learning plan that would instruct the students about certain eras or traditions.

One of the best ways of catching the student's attention, of actually persuading a young person to take on the adventure of aesthetic culture, is to approach it through those classic works that seem to have immediate appeal to a wide audience, works such as Beethoven's Fifth Symphony or *Moonlight Sonata,* Tchaikovsky's First Piano Concerto, or Rachmaninoff's Second or Third Piano Concertos; Orff's *Carmina Burana,* Stravinsky's *The Firebird,* or even the *Rite of Spring*; Rembrandt's, van Gogh's, Gauguin's, or Picasso's paintings; and in the literary sphere, fairy tales, Hemingway, Tolkien, and Orwell. And the biographical approach, which makes the great creators human, is certainly the best to start with.[16]

Of course, it is difficult for those well versed in music, art, and literature to return with enthusiasm to some of these works, most of which have become overfamiliar, but teachers should not forget the excitement with which they themselves first experienced them, and what worlds they opened up for exploration whenever that magical encounter happened. It is much better to promote works that may be well-known, but that also have integrity, profundity, energy, colour, charm — the sheer power of communication. Such elements are what keep audiences entranced, and these qualities will attract students. Why opt for, or let the students wallow in, the tired products of middlebrow culture, which are merely accessible and well marketed? Why opt for politically correct choices at the expense of expressiveness?

My argument is that enthusiasm, once generated, would motivate the student to work harder to master the intellectual background, the historical traditions, and other aspects (yes, including the political) of the works that have made an impact on him or her. Creative curiosity is admirable, but most people, and especially young people, only burn to know more about the things that matter to them. The reason that young people drown themselves in popular culture is not only peer pressure; some of it "turns them on" because it speaks directly of passion and energy and rebellion, and that is what aesthetic culture can do, provided the emotional side, the powerfully communicative side, of certain classics is not scorned or killed by pedantic or jaded teaching.

I doubt if I would have developed an interest in opera as early as I did had I not seen Gian Carlo Menotti's *The Consul* during the height of the cold war; once I became aware that opera could deliver an emotional punch, that it could have contemporary relevance, once I felt that I could understand what was happening on stage, be thrilled by the wedding of significant words to strong music, I was hooked – and willing to be patient with more challenging (and ultimately more rewarding) operas later on.

Positive, enthusiastic experience, and the will to learn, go hand in hand, and only later – and much less importantly – comes the possibility of participation. (I am not talking about custom-educated kids, prodigies, and natural talents in the arts.) The participatory side is not generally so important because we can have a very healthy culture where there are only a few creators and a large audience, though obviously it is better to have an audience that has some hands-on experience with the arts, because it is more likely that no mystique will stand in the way of appreciation and support. Of course, demystification does not banish wonder; it heightens it, for it dissolves the false aura that surrounds the arts and reveals their true mystery, which is their power – without being "life" – to reflect, reveal, and deepen our responses to, and illuminate the most important aspects of, life.

There are other important reasons to encourage participation in the arts among high school and university students. For one thing we know that the arts constitute an excellent mode of developing learning and life skills in both a very specific and a usefully broad sense. We need no longer be victimized by technological conceptions of what constitutes intelligence; it is not even necessary to refer to right-brain/left-brain constructs to emphasize the power of the contextual, textured, multifaceted experience of art, which returns us to a matrix without which our intelligence becomes both facile and unreal. Art, in fact, promotes the widest and deepest kind of knowing; by dwelling in a significant artwork, we expand our minds, develop our senses, engage ourselves wholly in learning and changing, and get a glimpse, sometimes, of rare and valuable vistas of the spirit. As the philosopher and scientist Michael Polanyi points out, when the artwork appeals to us, "we make it our own and clarify our lives by it. Art moves us, therefore, by influencing the lived quality of our existence."[17]

It is not possible any longer to make distinctions between the arts and sciences that suggest the location of vague inspiration or feeling or chaotic impulse in the former and precision and logical procedure in the latter. As Polanyi puts it,

> the artist's work is a constant invention of means for expressing his aims, coupled with a readjustment of his aims in the light of his means. This manner of deliberate growth resembles scientific or technical inquiry in sometimes offering opportunities for sudden inspiration and at other times demanding the taking of infinite pains. . . . The arts are imaginative representations, hewn into artificial patterns; and these patterns, when jointly integrated with an important content, produce a meaning of distinctive quality.[18]

When I first began to run fiction-writing workshops, I was under the impression that though my work with participants (our shared learning experience) might help them (and me) to write better fiction, it was unlikely to have broader effects. In fact, my writers have in many cases become better all-round students, more companionate learners, open to other points of view, better readers, far better critics and analysts. They also developed a better sense of how literary culture (and thus aesthetic culture in general) fits into (or doesn't fit into) contemporary life. It is clear from much modern theory that the creative process in art is closely related to that process in other spheres of activity. To neglect arts training is to leave undeveloped areas of sensibility, skill, and imagination that have wide implications for our general social progress. As *The Common Curriculum* document states, "The skills and aesthetic judgment that students develop through their study of the arts can be applied in many other areas of endeavour and will enrich their perception and enjoyment of many of the experiences they will encounter in daily life."[19]

Despite these observations some readers may perceive a problem. They may feel that the gap I have introduced between the aesthetic culture that I want to defend and the entertainment culture that surrounds us is an artificial one. Although I've already alluded to this problem in chapter 4, let me suggest a few additional points relating to it, points that touch on the question of education.

All of us who try to keep informed about the arts know that in the nineties it is no longer possible to understand aesthetic culture, "serious" culture, without being aware of the many ways in which it makes use of, transforms, plays with, alludes to, or interacts with what used to be called "low," "middlebrow," or "popular" culture – the whole complex area that I have referred to as "the entertainment culture." One of the delights of postmodernism, in fact, is this breaking down of barriers, this mixing of approaches. I am not referring merely to such explicit phenomena as pop art, third-stream music, new-wave science fiction, contemporary mystery writing, and video art, but to the whole mood and tone of our culture, where the old boundaries are being challenged everywhere by new approaches, new mixes of style addressed to a changing audience.

It is possible, in fact, to speak (epigrammatically and alliteratively) of contemporary culture as both *liminal* and *ludic* – liminal because our culture is a boundary-breaking enterprise, where the artist, it seems, must attempt every possible mix of style and tone; and ludic because much of the spirit of art today is playful: serious but nonsolemn, ironic but not always in the name of detachment, allusive and referential, although mainly for the purpose of finding some new perspective on the craziness of our world.[20]

It would be the worst kind of foolishness for educators to forget that young people are growing up in just such a world, with just such an approach to the arts and culture. To assume that the purpose of training in aesthetic or high culture is to insulate the student from these complexities is to doom the training to failure from the start.

But here a huge problem arises, because the very lightness, deftness, playfulness, and allusiveness of much contemporary art seems to exhibit, or invite, a nonserious (perhaps even mocking) attitude to the traditional aesthetic culture. Yet much of today's culture is still being created by artists with a deep involvement in the past, with great knowledge of the classic traditions. If young people are allowed to think that they can adopt the contemporary manner without a basic understanding of the past, without some knowledge of our great traditions, then they will be sadly deluded. Things are bad enough, but they can only get worse if we don't insist on continuity. We can take it for granted that young people will find ways to relate the traditional culture to whatever turns them on in contemporary art. But if they know nothing, or are allowed to get away with cheap mockeries or callow dismissals of what they don't understand, then they will have nothing to connect to, nothing to allude to, no basis from which to work. They will be completely at the mercy of the half-baked, the superficial, the clever; they will fall victim to the seductive and sinister sides of our entertainment culture. In the end, then, it is not a question of studying Beethoven to understand John Cage (though there is nothing wrong with that), or of studying Beethoven to woo the student away from listening to rock or jazz. It is rather a question of studying Beethoven (or Bach or Haydn, or Shakespeare or Tolstoy, or Rembrandt or Gauguin) to understand and dwell in works that manifest quality, complexity, emotional richness, and energy at the highest level, works that speak as part of a tradition, but newly to us as we encounter them. The study of our great cultural progenitors may help to make clear why certain current music, or plays or novels or poetry, why certain paintings – indeed, why certain rock bands or videos or multimedia shows – are better than others. It will suggest a better perspective on our present life and values, and show us (as a society) how to move toward the future, in ways that are creative and novel.

Education, however reformed, energized, or enlightened, is always only a partially successful solution to an infinitely complex and daunting problem: that of stimulating intellectual and emotional growth, of promoting social responsibility among a collectivity (and in order to achieve general results), even though you are dealing with an infinite variety of *individual* human needs, talents, and potentials.

There will always be children for whom a given method of education will not work, however eloquently it may be expressed in curriculum documents. (That is where the creative teacher comes in.) There will always be unpredictable moments of encounter (many of them outside the classroom) that will lead a child toward a creative life, perhaps of a kind unspecified in the programs thought up by the sometimes jaded (or theory-laden) adults who prescribe for her or him. That is why, above all, we need flexibility and constant vigilance against ends and means that are unduly rigid or ideologically fixed. And because education is a lifelong process, and should not stop with the schoolchild.[21] We must make sure that adults are encouraged to go on learning and changing and developing: insofar as we challenge ourselves, culture is challenged and enriched.

Conclusion: Arts and Culture in the Future of Canada

Civilization is a social order promoting cultural creation. Four elements constitute it: economic provision, political organization, moral traditions, and the pursuit of knowledge and the arts.
— Will Durant, *The Story of Civilization*

C ANADA APPROACHES THE 21st century with a well-defined national cultural profile, one that is increasingly visible around the world, and with an arts community of admirably varied accomplishments and consistent strength. Yet a sense of unease seems to grow, almost day by day, as changes occur and conflicts multiply: financial instability, organizational inflexibility, uncertainty about markets and audiences, ideological dissonance – all these are occurring at a time of rapid technological change, and seem to point to a somewhat less than glorious passage of our culture through the next several decades.

The keynote of this book is that Canada must have a healthy national culture in order to sustain itself in a world that is increasingly dominated by the American entertainment culture. Some might call this a nationalist position, but I am not a nationalist if that term suggests that culture exists chiefly to promote the state, or if it means that valid culture always (or chiefly) expresses the spirit of the nation, or that the arts and culture produced by individual artists are mysteriously linked to some national zeitgeist, without which they lack validity and reality.

When I look at history, I see various connections between art and nationalism. The nationalism that produces a work of art may be quite conscious and committed, and directed toward some historical purpose. Or the artist may create work in an atmosphere of national fervour, instinctively caught up in the energy of a region, a people, an emerging national spirit. Or the artistic enterprise may simply be seen in retrospect to carry something of a national spirit or tradition, even though the creator had other aims in view. Such diverse works as Goya's *The Disasters of War*, the poetry of the Young Germany movement of the early 19th century, the Russian nationalism evident in such a film as Eisenstein's *Alexander Nevsky*, the *Finlandia* of Sibelius, the operas of Verdi, the plays of Ibsen, or the poetry of Whitman give some idea of the range of possibilities.

Thanks to the Nazification of art in the nationalistic Third Reich and, on the other hand, to the particular concerns of modern criticism (which assumes the priority of the subjective, the interior, the symbolic form, the stylistic gesture, or the political orientation), nationalism tends to be suspect as a focus for art. Yet most art is produced by individuals with roots in some specific place, who share certain aspirations with similarly placed contemporaries, by artists who move to a universal level from a very deep commitment to their individual origins. As René Dubos puts it,

> Modern historical knowledge has confirmed that groups of people whom the accidents of history force to live together in a certain place tend to develop a body of shared ideas, values, and beliefs, which progressively becomes their ideal and guide. The culture they develop constitutes a whole which shapes itself as a continuously evolving national spirit.[1]

A writer, artist, or filmmaker may not have anything resembling a nationalist agenda (and in most cases shouldn't), but the creative spirit, however free, does not develop in a void. And when we put together a whole set of creative acts occurring over a certain period of time and in the context of a place, we can certainly speak of a "national spirit of art." As Dubos defines it, "Order is not imposed on the national genius from the outside; it evolves spontaneously as a structure of interrelationships generated by the constant interplay of its various elements."[2]

Art and culture must be understood as a genuine expression of the nation – indeed as a fundamental expression of what a nation is, has been, and can be. But official prescriptions and programs for artists are usually counterproductive, often deadly, because the creative spirit flourishes best in an atmosphere of freedom. There is a fine balance in all of this. If a state sets out its programs for culture too blatantly, then the worst kind of art is likely to result; if the state ignores art completely, then it invites barbarism.

Canada is a great modern democracy, but as such, and as a capitalistic society with strong egalitarian elements in its national makeup, as merely one "market" in the world's new technological network, it has to face some difficult underlying problems in relation to its arts and culture.

In a democracy the people themselves, the electorate, should presumably decide the issues that arise inevitably in the life of the state. We have elections to determine governments and policies; we may use referendums to decide issues of provincial sovereignty, church-state relations, capital punishment, and such matters. But do the people have a right to reject what might be construed as the basic elements that constitute a good society? Can we abolish the schools by a vote? Eliminate welfare, health services, old-age pensions? I would suggest that there are certain necessities, certain constituents of the social order, that cannot be dissolved, thrust away, or obliterated, even by a vote of the majority of the people. My argument for this is conservative in the old-fashioned sense (and, I would argue, in the *best* sense) of the word.

There are rights that we now assume to be part of our heritage and destiny as human beings who have set themselves apart from Darwinian nature; these rights form part of the social contract under which we take our place in society and perform our duties as citizens. We in Canada may not invoke such terminological inexactitudes as "life, liberty and the pursuit of happiness"; we may debate about the extent of such rights, about how they are to be applied, and about how we will pay for them, but we do not deny children education, or leave people to die in the streets. (Children *are* denied education, and people *do* die in the streets, but as a society we do not sanction this — not yet, anyway.)

It would be horrible to contemplate a society that rejected the elements of humane life, or that denied them to any number of its citizens. One of the most powerful forces for humane life, a component of civilized existence that, if we lost it, would shrivel our humanity, is the force of the arts and culture. They educate us to live in a human universe; they offer us values, visions, a sense of our own reality. They reconnect us with material things we may have forgotten, and provide an image of worlds, inner and outer, strange and familiar. The arts give us a vision of society, of the past, and of nature. They intrigue us with creative variations on ancient themes, allow us to live for a while in alternative worlds of someone's imagining; they entertain us. Consoling and enriching us, broadening perspectives and delighting the mind, the body, and the senses, the arts produce a knowledge that can lead to wisdom (sad, joyful, and sometimes terrifying). They may evoke anger or resignation, pity, tolerance, wonder, or simply mobilize our energies by refreshing our souls, but in any case they do more than any other human activity to define and celebrate life.

We do not have the right to abolish our official arts and culture, not even by a majority vote in our democracy. The majority that voted in

· 139 ·

Conclusion:
Arts and
Culture in the
Future of
Canada

favour of such a possibility would be comprised of those most in need of the transformation the arts and culture promise. It would be a majority manipulated by cynics and opportunists, or created by the failure of society to fulfill other parts of the social contract. It would be a starving majority, a sick majority, an uneducated majority, a majority deprived of the most fundamental material necessities and rendered incapable of soul making by evil and unnecessary circumstances.

Our Canadian democracy, as a capitalistic society, gives free rein to the inventiveness and enterprise that have making money as their object, but economic freedom, the market economy, if sanctioned and indulged without limit, may threaten the more fundamental rights of citizens. Education, health, welfare, culture, and art – these basic things, without which life would be intolerable – must be protected from the failures or excesses of a society that accepts capitalism as the least harmful form of economic life. People should not die because doctors refuse to treat them unless they can pay. Students should not be denied education because the universities are not money-making institutions and cannot afford to let them attend for nothing. A country should not lose its great museums, art galleries, theatres, symphony orchestras, and ballet companies because politicians perceive no pressure from their constituents to fund them, or because the private sector refuses to do so.

The arts cannot be left completely at the mercy of the free-market economy. If we stop supporting our individual artists, if we cut them off completely, creative work would not cease; books would still be written and pictures painted, but some people who should be encouraged to create would not, and we would be the losers. If we stop supporting our cultural institutions, many of them will die, and that would be a national tragedy, not because all Canadians would miss them (some, presumably, would not) but because Canada itself could not survive. In the wake of such a disaster our environment might seem unchanged, our politics would be similar, our boundaries would surely remain intact, yet sensitive people living in what remains of Canada would have lost all heart, all focus, all sense of themselves as being part of a coherent historical story. As for the insensitive, they would become invisible, falling into the limbo of the universal entertainment culture, which is concocted for everybody, and for nobody, and which eats souls without discrimination.

It is in a country's interest to support the arts and culture; first, to ensure national survival, but beyond that, as a validation of its history and the life of its people. Great nations are not the only way of providing people with the necessaries of life. Yet nations exist, not only to guarantee a minimum existence but also to provide coherence and meaning for their citizens, and to give expression to the life and destiny of their people. And what a country makes, does, and celebrates in its culture, *by means of its culture and arts,* determines its place in history and among the family of humankind. Clearly it is not merely a matter of winning at the Olympics and in the international hockey tournaments; it is really a question of creating something of more permanent value, what the ancient Greeks called "an imperishable possession."

Modern democracies have sometimes been suspicious of aesthetic culture because it seems beyond the reach of many. The credo of democracy, that all citizens are equal, seems to be contradicted by the hierarchies of talent and taste that we take for granted in the arts. Some people *are* more gifted than others, more knowledgeable, yes, but some people are also richer than others, some people happier by nature, stronger, more beautiful, and so on. All that can be guaranteed in a democracy is a rough equality of opportunity; that not everyone can play Beethoven sonatas, or even appreciate them, is no reason to question their value for everyone. (Yes, even those who aren't listening get some reward, not least the benefit of living in a society in which some islands of sanity and beauty exist amid the clamour, the false dazzle, the nonevents that mark modern life.) We should not pay attention to those who tell us that the arts are elitist, who cry "democracy" and mean by it the equality of mediocrity. Some politicians refer to democracy as if it were a cynical conspiracy between themselves and the electorate to ensure the triumph of the lowest common denominator.

If Canada is to enter the new century with a renewed energy, with the certainty of survival as a cultural entity, fundamental changes should be made; I have suggested a few possibilities in the previous pages. The Canadian sense of nationhood is perhaps stronger than many think. It is not contradicted by but rests on, I believe, local, regional, and provincial experience, the experience of many diverse groups that look from their diversity to the overriding fact of Canada. To the extent that we have valued both our local and our national perspectives, to the extent that we have wanted to shake ourselves out of complacency and routine thinking and into sharp new perceptions of what we are, the arts and culture have served us well. Yet Canadian confidence has been undermined, weakened by much that has happened in the political and economic life of the past decade. There is a new reality, confusing, sometimes threatening, yet we will understand it better, and deal with it in a finer spirit, if we have our artists to help us. It is time to acknowledge the true power of the arts and culture to enliven and energize our thinking, to provide vision and perspective, to help us integrate the past with the present, to show us our many possible futures.

We should move quickly toward a finer integration of the arts and culture into the everyday lives of Canadians; we should simplify structures, build on what we have, and find new means to help create and pass on the authentic spirit of Canada to future generations.

Notes

Introduction

1. Peter White of the Task Force on Professional Training for the Cultural Sector in Canada (1991), 109, qtd. and discussed in R. D. McIntosh, et al., *The State of the Art: Arts Literacy in Canada* (Victoria: Beach Holme, 1993) 84-86. See also the task force report, Canada, *Art Is Never a Given: Professional Training in the Arts in Canada* (Ottawa: Department of Supply and Services, 1991) 11-12. Matthew Arnold's idea of culture not only as the power of open-minded criticism but also as a familiarity with "the best that has been thought and said" underlies the idea of "high culture," which has become a target of leftist "democratizers," who regard it as a class ideal, as a genteel mask for the evils of bourgeois self-aggrandizement.

2. See Steven Globerman, *Cultural Regulation in Canada* (Montreal: Institute for Research on Public Policy, 1983) 60, 33. Globerman's conclusions are mind boggling in that they revive the barbarity of the Benthamites, who argued that pushpin (a trivial game) was as valuable an activity as poetry. Globerman suggests that the *only* case for government intervention in the arts is based on the "meritocracy" notion that "some tastes are better than others." He asserts that in Canada arts funding occurs because "a relatively small group of beneficiaries manipulate the political process to the disadvantage of the majority." Clearly conceptions of the good society are here reduced to a utilitarianism that one would think outdated even in the 19th century. That a society might have goals other than efficiency seems not to occur to Globerman. That the arts provide social cohesion, that they offer ideals of beauty and create possibilities of individual and social transformation by stimulating creative thinking, that they fulfill the universal societal need for celebratory rituals and mythical exemplars, that they serve as occasions of community integration, that they offer modes of expression to sharpen intelligence and discriminate feeling – none of this seems to have occurred to Globerman. It would require a Dickens to satirize such obtuse and idiotic materialism.

3. Globerman 39.

4. John Metcalf, *Freedom from Culture: Selected Essays, 1982-92* (Toronto: ECW, 1994) 38.

5. Tim Rowse comments: "Excellence reverberates with that bourgeois utopianism in which money and political power are politely separated from the higher things

in life such as art. . . . Excellence is a language of the powerful, which effaces the social basis of that power" (*Arguing the Arts: The Funding of Arts in Australia,* Ringwood, Austral.: Penguin, 1985, 33). The Marxist jargon is here self-exposed. "Excellence" is an ideal that has been shared by creative people knowledgeable in their crafts or arts throughout the ages and without regard to their social position. Excellence is a natural goal in one's work and critical judgements. It is an expression of the healthy tendency to seek connoisseurship in what one masters. A composer who attempts to write a symphony grapples with problems that allow him or her to understand better the genius of Beethoven or Sibelius; it becomes clear why they are cultural icons: they did it better. Bourgeois inflation takes second place to the Marxist capacity to manipulate both art and truth to satisfy social dogmas, to prop up ideas that events have suggested belong on the rubbish heap of history. See also John Pick, who attacks British genteel culture (*The Privileged Arts,* London: City Arts Series, n.d.); and S. M. Crean, who bristles at the elitism of the most prestigious Canadian arts institutions (*Who's Afraid of Canadian Culture?* Don Mills, ON: General, 1976).

6. See Allan Bloom, *The Closing of the American Mind* (Chicago: U of Chicago P, 1987) 62-81; Harold Bloom, *The Western Canon: The Books and School of the Ages* (New York: Harcourt, 1994) 517-28; and Neil Postman, *Technopoly: The Surrender of Culture to Technology* (New York: Vintage, 1993) ch. 11.

Chapter 1: The Introverted Culture and the Great Awakening

1. John Gray, "A Distinctive National Culture," *The Cultural Imperative: Creating New Management of the Arts,* ed. Shirley Ann Gibson, proc. of a conference, Kitchener-Waterloo, Nov. 1-3, 1985 (Toronto: Association of Cultural Executives, 1985) 134.

2. Gray 134.

3. Gray 134.

4. See Paul Litt, who suggests that Massey *created* the culture lobby in Canada (*The Muses, the Masses and the Massey Commission,* Toronto: U of Toronto P, 1992) 248. Litt defines the Massey elitism as a traditionalist reaction to American mass culture, and points out the Massey indifference to "progressive" art (249-53). See also Claude Bissell, *The Massey Report and Canadian Culture,* The John Porter Memorial Lecture (Ottawa: Carleton U, 1982) 18-19; Robert Fulford, "The Canada Council at Twenty-Five," *Saturday Night* Mar. 1982; J. L. Granatstein, "The Anglocentrism of Canadian Diplomacy," *Canadian Culture: International Dimensions,* ed. Andrew Senton Cooper, Contemporary Affairs Ser. 50 (Toronto: Centre on Foreign Policy and Federalism, 1985) 27-43; and George Woodcock, *Strange Bedfellows: The State and the Arts in Canada* (Vancouver: Douglas and McIntyre, 1985) 50-52.

5. Canada, *Report of the Royal Commission on National Development in the Arts, Letters, and Sciences, 1949-51* [i.e., the Massey Report] (Ottawa: Department of Supply and Services, 1957) 225.

6. Massey Report 274.

7. But the lines between "public" and "private" were often blurred. See Milton C. Cummings, Jr., and Richard S. Katz, *The Patron State: Government and the Arts in Europe, North America and Japan* (New York: Oxford UP, 1987) 3-16.

8. Gray 135.

9. Gray 137.

10. John Ralston Saul, "Culture and Foreign Policy," in Canada, *Report of the Special Joint Committee Reviewing Canadian Foreign Policy: The Position Papers* (Ottawa:

Public Works and Government Services, 1994) 85. See also Gilliane Mackay, "Canadian Books Flourish Abroad," *Maclean's* Oct. 3, 1988.

11. Saul 86.

12. *Culture and the Marketplace, Ideas,* CBC Radio (Toronto: CBC Radioworks, 1993) 12. See also Gerald Bonnot, who suggests that between 1933 and 1960 (when free secondary education was introduced in France), the cultural level didn't rise; the educational level merely declined ("French Cultural Policy: Evolution and Current Issues," in Aspen Institute, *The Arts, Economics and Politics,* Aspen, CO: Papers of the Aspen Institute, 1975, 28).

13. *Minutes of the Proceedings and Evidence of the Standing Committee on Communications and Culture,* Apr. 11, 1991, Issue 21 (Ottawa: Department of Supply and Services, 1991) 38.

Chapter 2: Arts, Media, and the Irresistible Future

1. Wilson Dizard, Jr., *Old Media, New Media* (New York: Longman, 1994) 30-33.

2. Marshall McLuhan, *Understanding Media: The Extensions of Man* (New York: Signet, 1967) 218.

3. Dizard 171.

4. McLuhan 75.

5. Richard Saul Wurman, *Information Anxiety* (New York: Doubleday, 1989) chs. 1, 7.

6. Although a National Endowment for the Arts study seems to deny this, I have been told as much by so many people that I doubt the study. See McIntosh et al. 73. Much more convincing is the finding of the Decima researchers that "falling in love with a work of art" is one of the most influential factors in getting a consumer to make a ticket, book, or record purchase. See *The Canadian Arts Consumer Profile: 1990-1991* (Toronto: Decima Research; Les consultants culture, 1992) xxiii.

7. Dizard 182.

8. Ross Eaman, "Canadian Broadcasting Corporation," *The Canadian Encyclopedia,* 1988 ed.; Paul Rutherford, "Radio Programming," *The Canadian Encyclopedia,* 1988 ed.

9. Morris Wolfe, *Jolts: The TV Wasteland and the Canadian Oasis* (Toronto: Lorimer, 1985) 132. Despite his often trenchant critique, Wolfe, in my opinion, greatly overrates CBC Television.

10. Tony Atherton, "TV Nation: World Tunes in on Canada's Television Set," *Ottawa Citizen* June 30, 1995.

11. Peter Harcourt, "Film," *The Canadian Encyclopedia,* 1988 ed.

12. Incomprehensibly the CBC failed utterly to make use of Canadian cinema to introduce French Canada to English viewers, or to program much English cinema in Quebec. And sadly, in the nineties, Telefilm Canada and the NFB have become points of skirmish in the battle over separation. Some Quebec politicians have demanded that these agencies be kicked out of the province, to which some critics in English Canada have chanted "Amen!" See Peter Pearson, "Move NFB, Telefilm out of Quebec Now," *Gazette* [Montreal] Feb. 9, 1991.

13. Gage was later bought by a Canadian company. It is now owned by the Canadian Publishing Corporation, which also owns Macmillan Canada.

14. "The Advent of the World Book," *Economist* Dec. 26, 1967: 109-13; Gayle Feldman, "The Anatomy of an Acquisition," *Publisher's Weekly* June 26, 1987; July 3, 1987. For the effect of some of these changes on the Canadian novel in recent years, see Stephen Henighan, "Writing in Canadian: Problem of the Novel," *Hungarian Studies in English* 21 (1990): 79-85.

15. A similar if less jarring process is happening in the new mass media, where huge corporate moves are made in the belief that only media giants "can absorb failures and wait for the high returns from more successful products." These firms want to control a range of services they can market "in ways that would provide profitable synergies among their products" (see Dizard 178). The emphasis here, as in the publishing industry, is on profits and corporate balance rather than on content, and we may doubt that a cultural nirvana awaits us around the next media corner.

Chapter 3: The Arts on Television, and Other Mind-numbing Pleasures

1. Tony M. Lentz, "The Medium Is the Madness: Television and the Pseudo-Oral Tradition in America's Future," *Communications and the Future,* ed. Howard F. Didsbury, Jr. (Bethesda, MD: World Future Society, 1982) 323-25.

2. See Guy Lyon Playfair, *The Evil Eye: The Unacceptable Face of Television* (London: Cape, 1990). Despite some irrelevant asides and opinion mongering, he makes telling points about the evils of television: for example, viewers do not control the medium; they end up hating themselves for their enforced passivity (47-48). (Many viewers will agree.) Myopia, malnutrition, speech disorders, obesity, and antisocial behaviour may be side effects of television addiction (48). TV may actually hypnotize ardent viewers; they have strong alpha waves; their brains are in a "slow" state, yet are bombarded with images and are thus unduly receptive (56). We don't remember what we see on TV, but are affected by its emotional violence (110-11). Playfair also reports on the Williams study in British Columbia, which surveyed a town before and after the advent of television. Community participation and reading skills suffered as young people became "mentally passive" (145-48). See also Jerry Mander, who sees television as highly addictive and trance inducing (*Four Arguments for the Elimination of Television,* New York: Morrow, 1978). Neil Postman's demolitions of television on cultural grounds are both magisterial and funny; see *Amusing Ourselves to Death: Public Discourse in the Age of Show Business* (New York: Penguin, 1985); and *Technopoly.*

3. Choosing baseball as my example has some point. McLuhan 284 argues plausibly that baseball belongs to the past, to the era of the hot press, "hot mommas, jazz babies, of sheiks and shebas, of vamps and gold-diggers and the fast buck." He predicts its demise in the television era – not a bad prediction, judging by the recent lack of fan enthusiasm. From this perspective all the electronic media "hype" surrounding the ballpark game today could be seen as a desperate ploy to "filter" the game and make it acceptable to a society that would otherwise regard it as a fossilized ritual.

4. Art galleries, however, are more threatened by "on-line" viewing of their collections. Raves about the "convenience" of having art on the computer overlook the fact that these similitudes are very poor versions of the originals. This may not change. In 1995 I attended the marvellous Symbolist Exhibition at the Musée des Beaux Arts in Montreal. I walked into a room and was thrilled by a sudden flare of yellow (as of sunflowers and daffodils) in the flowing dress of Gauguin's *Young Christian Girl.* When I got home and looked at the picture in my copy of the exhibition's expensive illustrated volume, I saw, to my disappointment, that the yellow shown there was quite different, duller, more earthbound and boring. If books can't do it, how can we expect the computer or television screen to give us an accurate picture of great art? See Phil Patton, "The Pixels and Perils of Getting Art On-Line," *New York Times* Aug. 7, 1994, sec. 2. Gallery reference rooms with computer art files sound all very well, but inevitably they will further erode the face-to-face experience of art.

5. Neil Postman, "Remembering the Golden Age," *Conscientious Objections: Stirring up Trouble About Language, Technology and Education* (New York: Knopf, 1988) 116-27.

6. Donald R. Vroon, "Concert versus Record," *American Record Guide* July-Aug. 1995: 56-57. Vroon (the editor of this noted record-reviewing medium) makes an excellent case for live performance. Cf. McLuhan 247: "With hi-fi, the phonograph meets the TV tactile challenge."

7. Vroon 56.

8. René Dubos, *A God Within* (New York: Scribner's, 1972) 58.

9. I am thinking of John Keats's reference to this life as a "vale of soul-making," and of the psychologist James Hillman's notion of soul making.

10. See Daniel J. Czitrom, *Media and the American Mind* (Charlotte: U of North Carolina P, 1982) ch. 6; and B. F. Powe, *A Climate Charged* (Toronto: Mosaic, 1984) 25.

11. Tim Page, ed., *The Glenn Gould Reader* (Toronto: Lester, 1984) 99.

12. Page 246.

13. In a letter to me (June 26, 1978), Gould complained of Yehudi Menuhin's "constitutional" inability to follow a prepared text. An example of Gould's desire for perfection and control? Gould is an amazing and always intriguing figure, but to get beyond Canadian Gouldolatry, one must read Andrew Kazdin's powerful account, which portrays something of the darker side of Gould. See Kazdin, *Glenn Gould at Work: Creative Lying* (Boston: Little, Brown, 1984).

14. See Donald R. Vroon, "The Cruelty of Reviewing," *American Record Guide* July-Aug. 1995: 57-59.

15. Derrick de Kerckhove, *The Skin of Culture* (Toronto: Somerville, 1994) ch. 2.

16. Barrie Sherman and Phil Judkins, *Glimpses of Heaven, Visions of Hell: Virtual Reality and Its Implications* (London: Hodder, 1992) 196-206. The authors waver between enthusiastic acceptance of the new medium and a sense of its triviality and, despite that, its potential for evil. Words and phrases such as "addiction," "a virus," "absolute power," and "a dictator's dream" appear frequently; the writers also seem to imply (what may well be true) that for most people the only really interesting part of VR is the possibility of virtual sex. Despite the seemingly discriminating enthusiasm of writers such as de Kerckhove, it is perhaps significant that science fiction, which has dealt extensively with the kinds of changes predicted by these media futurists, has portrayed the social effects in an extremely negative way. The exception? The naive American pro-technological SF of the forties "golden age."

17. *Culture and the Marketplace* 65. The new media art is by no means a unique phenomenon in history. It is simply the latest example of the "technological" form or means becoming the focus when it reaches a critical point of inventiveness, while lacking significant new content. Most analogous to our current obsession with technology as salvation, our sense of it as a virtual reality, are the mystery religions of the late Roman Empire (fourth century A.D.), which used elaborate technologies (rather than creative new doctrines) to woo and dazzle the devotee. Although such religions had existed for a long time, "technological tricks" made them newly popular. Theoretically open to all, they became the provenance of a few devotees who experienced the "virtual reality" of the mysteries. In elaborate rituals devotees gave up the ordinary day, entered the darkness, experienced sound, light, and auditory wonders (written text was limited or nonexistent), and underwent initiations, which involved the manipulation of technology by experts. The ordinary world was left behind for a promise of immortality. All of this disappeared when a truly creative new doctrine of great simplicity and universal appeal appeared, namely Christianity. See Jacob Burckhardt, *The Age of Constantine the Great* (New York: Pantheon, 1949) 166, 173; and Marvin W. Meyer, *The Ancient Mysteries: A Sourcebook* (New York: Harper, 1987).

Chapter 4: Arts or Entertainment

1. Dizard 4-5; Richard M. Dorson, *Folklore and Folklife* (Chicago: U of Chicago P, 1972) 41-45.

2. Allan Gotlieb, "Canada in the 1990s: The Canadian Cultural Challenge." Speech delivered to the Junior Achievement of Metro Toronto and York Region Board of Governor's Dinner. Nov. 8, 1990.

3. Robert Jewett and John Shelton Lawrence, *The American Monomyth* (New York: Anchor, 1977) 219-20.

4. John Bell, *Guardians of the North: The National Superhero in Canadian Comic Book Art* (Ottawa: National Archives of Canada, 1992) 3. The "Canadian superhero" was a direct imitation of the American, an example in itself of importation of content.

5. J. Russell Harper, "Folk Art," *The Canadian Encyclopedia,* 1988 ed.

6. In the course of a vigorous celebration of the distinctness of Canadian culture, Pierre Berton lists a number of Canadian popular artists. No one could dispute his choices (and he might well have added his own name), yet some of the artists he cites produce work that is indistinguishable from American work, work saturated with American values. Many Americans would not think of them as Canadian at all. Whatever the artistic value of their work, they are at best (and only very indirectly) cultural assets. See McIntosh et al. 90-91. In discussing "the perilous myth of cultural industries," George Woodcock reminds us of how commercialism defeats art (see 131-39). Yet this distinction still eludes many. For some blithe assumptions of "Canadian is Canadian, whatever the content," see Damian Isherwood, "Stop Selling Canadian Culture, Hollywood Lawyer Tells Filmmakers," *Ottawa Citizen* Oct. 7, 1995; and Mike Boone, "Much Musing: In Mexico, Finland, MuchMusic Plants the Flag Nicely," *TV Times* July 1-7, 1995: 7.

7. A grateful nation gave the nationalist Sibelius a pension for life; Tolstoy was deemed "a great writer of the Russian people"; at Verdi's funeral the crowds spontaneously broke into song (what they sang was "Va, pensiero," his chorus of the Hebrew slaves from *Nabucco:* Italians felt that that music reflected their own longing for a free and united Italy). Recently, when an ad firm used a parody of a famous scene from a Fellini film on Italian television, there was an outcry of protest from the public.

8. Richard Slotkin, *Regeneration Through Violence: The Mythology of the American Frontier, 1600-1860* (Middletown, CT: Wesleyan UP, 1973) 14-24.

9. Jewett and Lawrence 169-73; 195-96.

10. Reinhold Niebuhr, *The Irony of American History* (London: Nisbet, 1952) 30-34.

11. Jewett and Lawrence 185.

12. The idea of Canada as a postmodern country was first developed by journalist Richard Gwynn in a lecture at Brock University in 1994. See Michael Valpy, "'Button Your Lip,' Says Mrs. Finestone," *Globe and Mail* [Toronto] Nov. 29, 1994.

13. See John Keats, *Selected Poems and Letters* (New York: Houghton Mifflin, 1959) 261.

14. The high figures given in McIntosh et al. 349 fail to distinguish between aesthetic and popular culture. Almost all the coverage goes to popular entertainment.

Chapter 5: The Arts, the New Politics, and the Next Canada

1. Given the collapse of the Soviet Union, this may seem surprising. Was it simply the usual penchant of professors for lost causes? Did the disappearance of the mailed fist allow academics to indulge their free fantasies about socialism without the uncomfortable reminder of the gulags?

2. Harold Bloom, 15-41, 517-28; William A. Henry III, *In Defence of Elitism* (New York: Doubleday, 1994) 158-94.

3. See "The Canada Council and Cultural Diversity," in-house paper of the Canada Council, 1993. The word *multiculturalism,* used almost universally now in Canada and the United States, is a journalistic catchall for a phenomenon that might be better (though not so mellifluously) designated *multiethnicism.* Canada is multicultural because it has two cultures: Québécois and Anglo; it is multiethnic because it has many immigrants who wish to assert the cultural value of their own traditions. See Wayne Roberts, "Measuring Multiculturalism's Misunderstanding," *Now* Nov.-Dec. 1994. Roberts points out provocatively and shrewdly that Canadian multiculturalism invites assimilation, whereas the American "melting pot" concept hasn't. Multiculturalism doesn't cause the ghetto experience – which is a natural part of immigration. Cultures, he suggests, need diversity; monoculture is stifling. One can agree with all this, yet feel that ethnic agendas are too divisive and set up in a needless and sometimes opportunistic way vis-à-vis the main culture. See also Metcalf 107-28, who argues that writers outside the "Anglo" tradition were certainly coming to the fore, but that the government unfortunately blundered in with "official" support. "Unlike the bureaucrats I am content to wait for these writers to emerge," Metcalf writes (127).

4. Stephen Godfrey, "Canada Council Asks Whose Voice Is It Anyway," *Globe and Mail* [Toronto] Mar. 21, 1992. Zemans's obfuscating word in the interview was "consultation" – artists have to "consult" minorities if they wish to receive a grant from the Council in order to write about them. Could anything reveal more clearly the perils of bureaucratic control of the arts? Consultation is appropriate for bureaucracies, perhaps, but clearly absurd for creative artists.

5. *Globe and Mail* [Toronto] Mar. 28, 1995. Predictably activists such as Susan Crean once again demonstrated their grim ideological fix by jumping in to defend the censorship.

6. Joyce Zemans, interview with Peter Gzowski, *Morningside,* Apr. 1, 1992. See also Zemans's letter, *Globe and Mail* [Toronto] Apr. 4, 1992.

7. "The Canada Council and Cultural Diversity" 2.

8. "The Canada Council and Cultural Diversity" 2.

9. "The Canada Council and Cultural Diversity" 3.

10. Personal communication.

11. Personal communication.

12. "Minority Writers Conference Claims 'Revolutionary' Success," *Vancouver Sun* July 4, 1994.

13. Letter from the Council's Associate Director Brian Anthony to the *Globe and Mail* [Toronto] May 18, 1994; "Writers' Session Barring Whites Triggers Concerns," *Vancouver Sun* Apr. 7, 1994.

14. "Feds Won't Fund Writers' Workshop That Bars Whites," *Vancouver Sun* June 9, 1994; "Shouting Match Mars Forum on Writers' Union Conference," *Globe and Mail* [Toronto] May 14, 1994; see also Metcalf 123-24. Pierre Berton courageously attacked the position of the new racists and was himself booed and denounced as a racist, an incident that (understandably) hurt him deeply. See Val Ross, "Captain Canada at 75," *Globe and Mail* [Toronto] Oct. 7, 1995.

15. "Writers' Session Barring Whites Triggers Concerns," *Vancouver Sun* Apr. 7, 1994.

16. "Bread and Races: Writers' Union, Divided over Writing Thru Race Conference, Tries to Get Down to Business," *Quill and Quire* July 1994: 21; "Shouting Match Mars Forum on Writers' Union Conference," *Globe and Mail* [Toronto] May 14, 1994.

17. "Minority Writers' Conference Claims 'Revolutionary' Success," *Vancouver Sun* July 4, 1994.

18. Qtd. in "Pride and Prejudice: An Immigrant Author Says Multicultural Policy Creates Ethnic Ghettos," *Maclean's* Nov. 7, 1994: 34.

19. Mavor Moore, "Will Ayatollah's Curse Turn Multicultural Dream into Nightmare?," *Globe and Mail* [Toronto] Mar. 4, 1989; editorial, *Globe and Mail* [Toronto] Nov. 29, 1994. Note that until recently the contribution of immigrants to Canadian culture was accomplished without a constant assertion of "new agendas" or cries of persecution and exclusion. This list includes Tyrone Guthrie, Celia Franca, Gwenneth Lloyd, and Betty Farrally (England); Ludmilla Chiriaeff (Latvia); John Hirsch (Hungary); Herman Geiger-Torel (Germany); not to mention the many American musicians who moved up to play in Canadian orchestras. The idea that the "mainstream" culture was a club of "old boys" educated at Eton and Oxford (or Upper Canada College and Queen's) is sheer nonsense. As Canadian culture matured, nationalists began to object to constant imports of foreign talent; now some immigrants regard assimilation as capitulation – hardly a promising basis for a new synthesis.

20. "'Button Your Lip,' Says Mrs. Finestone," *Globe and Mail* [Toronto] Nov. 29, 1994.

21. Henry 211.

22. Much more to the point is Donald R. Vroon's observation: "*the greatest human achievements are transcendent – universal – they belong to all of us.* Beethoven belongs to black female music lovers as much as to white males. His greatness has nothing to do with subcultural sensibilities and values. His greatness is supercultural, maybe even a bit supernatural." Vroon adds: "is the Bible meaningful only to Jews? . . . Shall we dismiss the wisdom of Confucius? Are Japanese woodprints ugly to us because they speak of alien values? Is African song too 'foreign' for Americans to appreciate?" ("Classical Music and Multiculturalism," *American Record Guide* Jan.-Feb. 1993: 58-59).

23. Tennyson: "Better fifty years of Europe than a cycle of Cathay" ("Locksley Hall").

24. The virulent assault on academic freedom of speech from the left is a sad story in itself. In 1993-94 Bob Rae's Ontario NDP government put forth the notorious *Framework Regarding Prevention of Harassment and Discrimination in Ontario Universities,* a document that proposed (undefined) "zero tolerance" of (as it amounted to) any controversial opinions of professors and students, in or out of the classroom. "The Ontario government has banned free thought and expression at the very institutions devoted to such freedoms – our universities – and there has been no public outcry," wrote Peter Calamai in an editorial in the *Ottawa Citizen.* And John Fekete, Trent cultural studies professor, declared: "Zero tolerance comes from the Reagan era war on drugs. It literally means that universities would acquire a legal responsibility they cannot fulfill without destroying themselves" (Qtd. in Tim Lougheed, "How Far Is Too Far?," *University Affairs* 35.4 [1994]: 6-7). See also John Sopinka, "Freedom of Speech Under Attack," *University Affairs* 35.4 (1994): 13. Meanwhile we have the incredible confession of Jill Vickers, professor of Canadian studies at Carleton University, who brags about "turning in" one of her colleagues, who happened not to meet her self-proclaimed high ethical standards, and who supports in print the spying and harassment activities of one of her students against an apparently reputable colleague. ("Are Efforts to Renovate the Concept of Academic Freedom Useful?," Status of Women Suppl. *Canadian Association of University Teachers Bulletin* 41.6 [1994]: 7). By contrast, note the courageous outspokenness of Doreen Kimura, who suggests that complaints against professors are " too often . . . brought by disgruntled students who have not done well in a course." She specifies that "in two cases I know of the charges rested

entirely on the duration of eye contact (in one case felt to be too long, in the other too short!)" ("In Defence of Discomfort," *University Affairs* 36.1 [1995]: 15). We have the equally courageous opinion of David Rayside, a declared homosexual, who has written: "As someone who has sought, however modestly, to expand the curriculum by engaging issues of gender, sexual orientation, and race, I am not sure that I want to be a part of an institution that does not protect my right to teach what I want to teach" ("Heterosexism and Free Speech," *CAUT Bulletin* 40.8 [1993]). In fact the "antiharassment industry" in Canadian universities has grown out of all proportion. The budget for this dubious activity was (at the University of Toronto in 1995, for example) approximately $1.5 million, and very substantial elsewhere, which has not prevented outcomes such as the recent University of British Columbia fiasco, in which the administration, "acting without agreed procedures on how to handle charges of systemic discrimination... succeeded in tarnishing the reputation of an entire department" ("CAUT Response to the McEwen Report," *CAUT Bulletin* 42.7 [1995]: 6-8). See also Lesley Krueger, "A Few Are Influencing a Lot at UBC," *Globe and Mail* [Toronto] Oct. 6, 1995. Krueger asserts that "the McEwen report painted a grossly unbalanced picture... ." See also Mark Leiren-Young, "Incorrect Politics: Was UBC's Inquiry into Charges of Racism and Sexism a Step Backward?" *The Georgia Straight* Dec. 7-14, 1995: 13-25.

25. "Exhibit 'Deplorable': The *Into the Heart of Africa* Exhibit (Royal Ontario Museum) Is Under Fire Again," *Globe and Mail* [Toronto] July 28, 1990; "Injunction Orders Halt to Protests Near ROM," *Toronto Star* May 12, 1990.

26. Allan Gotlieb, "The Museum of Today: Challenges, Caveats and Respect for the Public," speech delivered to the Museum Trustee Association, Toronto, Oct. 1, 1992.

27. Robert Powell, "Indigena," *Muse* 10.4 (1993): 70.

28. Powell 71.

29. Powell 71.

30. "More Ammunition for War Series Debate," *Globe and Mail* [Toronto] Nov. 19, 1992.

31. Robert Fulford, "The Philistines Strike Back: How the NDP Crippled a Proud Art Gallery," *Financial Times* July 13-19, 1992.

32. Christopher Hume, "Politically Correcting the Arts," *Toronto Star* July 18, 1992.

33. Cultural relativism combined with the mostly shallow debunking of Freud, the tendency to throw out his great insights because of a few important (but hardly global) errors and exaggerations, has come near to making ours a society in which any kind of lunacy, neurosis, and self-indulgent nonsense can lay claim to intellectual and emotional respectability. On the University of British Columbia case, see Leiren-Young 13-16.

34. "Will Ayatollah's Curse Turn Multicultural Dream into Nightmare?" *Globe and Mail* [Toronto] Mar. 4, 1989.

35. For example, Susan Crean, a nationalist, feminist, and advocate of "democratic culture" (i.e., she considers aesthetic culture too elitist), as early as 1986 attacked aspects of multiculturalism that seemed to threaten her own ideology. Her opposition to multiculturalism is not that its cultural relativism undermines the traditional artistic culture; it is only that it sometimes upholds antifeminist and antinationalist agendas. See "Cracks in the Mosaic," *Border Crossings* 5.4 (1986): 9-11.

36. Harold Bloom passim.

37. See Leon Botstein, *Culture and the Market Place* 71-72.

38. Botstein 76.

39. We project our inner self-hatred, our unacknowledged evil, outward, as Hitler did in his hatred of the Jews. Cf. C. G. Jung's idea of "shadow projection" (*Aion: Researchers into the Phenomenology of the Self,* vol. 9, pt. 2 of *Collected Works,* Princeton: Princeton UP, 1959, 8-10).

40. In fact, it matters not a whit what their "philosophies" or politics were, whom they collaborated with or refused to collaborate with: what matters is the aesthetic power of their work. Harold Bloom writes: "The silliest way to defend the Western Canon is to insist that it incarnates all of the seven deadly moral virtues that make up our supposed range of normative values and democratic principles" (29).

41. Shakespeare's *The Taming of the Shrew* and *The Merchant of Venice* have, in effect, been banned from Stratford for political reasons. The Ottawa Shakespeare Festival in 1994 presented a "politically correct" version of the former which, gratifyingly, closed after a short run because a bored and indignant public stayed away in droves. Anyone who has seen this play produced by an intelligent and skilled company knows that it is possible to play "against the text" and make the piece delightfully contemporary in every sense.

Chapter 6: The Nature of the Crisis

1. Pierre Berton, interview with Pamela Wallin, CBC TV, Sept. 21, 1995; Simona Chiose, "The Best and Worst of Our Cultural Times," *Globe and Mail* [Toronto] Aug. 19, 1995.

2. "A Downward Cultural Spiral," *Ottawa Citizen* July 2, 1992; Victor Dwyer et al., "Culture in Crisis," *Maclean's* July 20, 1992; Max Wyman, "Arts Going Down the Drain and People Just Yawn," *The Province* [Vancouver] Jan. 20, 1991; Peter Pearson, "Funding Crisis at the Canada Council," *Ottawa Citizen* Oct. 20, 1990; Christopher Harris, "Performing Arts Companies Singing Subscription Blues," *Globe and Mail* [Toronto] Mar. 2, 1991; Tom Barrett, "Telefilm Funds in Freeze Frame," *Vancouver Sun* Feb. 27, 1991; Paule des Rivières, "Situation précaire aux Grands Ballets Canadien," *Le Devoir* [Montreal] Feb. 28, 1991; "Liberals Have Betrayed the CBC with Cuts," *Calgary Herald* Feb. 25, 1995. Total attendance for combined theatre, music, dance, and opera companies dropped from 15 million in 1988-89 to 14 million in 1992-93. The only group that improved its audience numbers in that time was opera. Figures quoted by Hester Riches, "Faith in the Future," *Vancouver Sun* Mar. 22, 1995.

3. Jamie Portman, "Fiscal Anemia Saps National Ballet," *Ottawa Citizen* Feb. 19, 1991; Max Wyman, "Arts Going Down the Drain and People Just Yawn," *The Province* [Vancouver] Jan. 20, 1991.

4. Jamie Portman, "Stratford's in Trouble," *Gazette* [Montreal] Feb. 2, 1991; Dwyer et al.

5. Jamie Portman, "Publishers Plead for Tax Breaks," *Ottawa Citizen* Oct. 30, 1991.

6. Jamie Portman, "Publishers Plead for Tax Breaks," *Ottawa Citizen* Oct. 30, 1991; Saul 88.

7. Small presses, in my experience, lack elementary marketing skills. Consider the case of a publisher (a good and reputable publisher, far above the average run of subsidized presses) who accepted a mystery novel from a Canadian writer, no doubt on the perfectly reasonable assumption that the firm might sell a few copies of a work in this popular genre. Their assumption proved false because (1) the writer resides overseas and could do no marketing, and (2) the publisher knew nothing about marketing mysteries, anyway. On the other hand, this publisher rejected a volume

of short stories by the same writer; this book was arguably far more creative and original, and much more of a contribution to Canadian literature than the mystery. It also could have been marketed more easily through the channels already known to the publisher. How does one justify a government subsidy in a case like this? How is a subsidy in this case (and there are many like them) serving Canadian culture? But small presses have other problems. Their handling of manuscripts is notoriously inefficient, and they are often *less* responsive to writers who have submitted work than are the major firms. They are often absurdly trendy, and inbreeding is the rule. A writer may be surprised to note, for example, that the same address applies whether you are submitting to *Poetry Canada,* Quarry Press, *Quarry Magazine,* or *Canadian Fiction Magazine. Not* reassuring. See Metcalf 24-25, who questions the cultural value of the subsidized Canadian presses.

8. Barrie McKenna and Val Ross, "U.S. Book Chain Setting Up Shop," *Globe and Mail* [Toronto] Nov. 24, 1995; and Val Ross, "Why U.S. Book Giants May Spell Disaster," *Globe and Mail* [Toronto] Dec. 2, 1995.

9. Richard King and Jack Stoddart, "Big American Booksellers Imperil Canadian Publishing Industry," *Vancouver Sun* Dec. 15, 1995.

10. "Who's Afraid of Bigger Bookstores?" Dec. 11, 1995.

11. Personal communication from Industry Canada.

12. Stephen Godfrey, "Artists Deserve a Hand," *Globe and Mail* [Toronto] Aug. 1, 1992.

13. Gotlieb, "Canada in the 1990s."

14. Gotlieb, "Canada in the 1990s."

15. It was perhaps inevitable, given its perilous balance between the state and the independent artist, that the Council should get into difficulty. See the prophetic essay by Frank Milligan, "The Ambiguity of the Canada Council," *Love and Money: The Politics of Culture,* ed. David Helwig (Ottawa: Oberon, 1990) 68-69. John Pick argues plausibly that government always seeks, in one way or another, to control the artists it supports (*Arts in a State* 127-28). See also Anthony Phillips, Introduction, Aspen Institute 15-16.

16. Charlotte Gray, "Donna in the Lion's Den," *Saturday Night* July-Aug. 1995: 19-24.

17. Val Ross, "Scale Down Art Bank, Advisory Team Says: Canada Council Questions Report," *Globe and Mail* [Toronto] Nov. 22, 1995.

18. Paula Gustafson, "Art Bank's Role Remains in Limbo," *The Georgia Straight* Dec. 7-14, 1995: 65.

19. Susan Riley, "Canada Council Urged to Take Quick Action on Future of Art Bank," *Ottawa Citizen* Nov. 24, 1995.

20. Stephen Godfrey, "Going Solo," *Globe and Mail* [Toronto] Feb. 9, 1991; Pearson; Susan Riley, "Cost of Leaving Could Jeopardize Quebec Arts Community," *Ottawa Citizen* Oct. 28, 1995.

21. Susan Riley, "Cost of Leaving Could Jeopardize Quebec Arts Community," *Ottawa Citizen* Oct. 28, 1995.

22. Christopher Harris, "CBC Cuts 639 Jobs Across Country," *Globe and Mail* [Toronto] Dec. 8, 1995; Editorial, *Globe and Mail* [Toronto] Nov. 23, 1995; Christopher Harris, "CBC's Shortwave Service to Be Killed," *Globe and Mail* [Toronto] Dec. 13, 1995.

23. I have spent many hours, years, listening to the BBC, to WQXR (New York), to WNYC (New York), to the various outlets of National Public Radio, to Norddeutsche Rundfunk, and other radio services. We need an "elite" radio service that incorporates some of the following features. (1) less rigorous time blocking for programs – an older custom, but a good one for arts stations. (2) more classical

music played without commentary and in longer time blocks – for example, three major works by a composer, in a two- or three-hour time period, rather than "balanced" programs in smaller slots. One gets to know music by hearing a great deal of it – the more variety the better. And the present "concert" arrangement means that some music we should hear never gets played. I hesitate to give examples – though I have plenty – because some testy C B C vice president, guarding the fortress, will write to me telling me, "But we *did* do such and such!" The point is that C B C is *not* doing some things it should do. (3) More input by freelancers, not just condescending requests for us "listeners" to write to R S V P and tell of our "musical experiences." When was the last time any commentator outside the small national in-group of "artsies" had a piece on *The Arts Tonight?* (4) More news about the arts in the excellent vein of *The Arts Report.* (Don't get me wrong; there are many things I *like* about C B C F M-stereo.)

24. See Sandy Stewart, "A Eulogy for C B C Television," *Globe and Mail* [Toronto] Nov. 11, 1995; Hester Riches, "Canadian Public Television: Not a Pretty Picture," *Vancouver Sun* Mar. 20, 1995.

25. Christopher Harris, "Cuts Will Sap C B C, Group Warns," *Globe and Mail* [Toronto] Dec. 6, 1995.

26. Christopher Harris, "On Board at the C B C," *Globe and Mail* [Toronto] Dec. 2, 1995.

27. Christopher Harris, "Group of Seven Campaigns to Save C B C," *Globe and Mail* [Toronto] Nov. 29, 1995.

28. "Feel Good Bulletins Add Insult to Injury at C B C," *Globe and Mail* [Toronto] Nov. 27, 1995.

29. Jay Stone, "Masse Report Deftly Ducks N A C Reform," *Ottawa Citizen* Feb. 26, 1991.

30. Janice Kennedy, "Keeping a Sacred Trust," *Ottawa Citizen* Feb. 26, 1995.

31. Ray Conlogue, "Arts Centre Director Resigns: Pennefather Cites Differing Views," *Globe and Mail* [Toronto] Dec. 19, 1995.

32. Jill Vardy, "C R T C Given Extra Work Without Any More Cash," *Financial Post* Feb. 11, 1991.

33. Darrel R. Skidmore, *Canadian-American Relations* (Toronto: Wiley, 1979) 82-83; personal communication from C B C music producer.

34. Saul 112-14.

35. Peter O'Neil, "Funds for Montreal Cultural Centre Raises Ire of B.C. Conservative MPs," *Vancouver Sun* Feb. 23, 1991; Frederic Tremblay, "Marcel Masse 'ne nous consulte pas, il nous informe' se plaint Liza Hébert," *La Presse* [Montreal] Feb. 27, 1991; Sid Adilman, "The Good News Is What We Know, the Bad News Is What We Don't," *Toronto Star* Feb. 23, 1991.

36. For example, *Minutes of the Proceedings and Evidence of the Standing Committee on Communications and Culture,* Apr. 10, 1990, Issue 8 (Ottawa: Department of Supply and Services, 1990).

37. See Woodcock ch. 14. See also Arnold Edinborough, "Cultural Review Is Awash in Inconsistencies and Gaps," *Financial Post* Nov. 27, 1982.

38. Saul 90.

Chapter 7: Artistic Culture

1. Carl-Johan Kleberg, "Cultural Policy in Sweden," Cummings and Katz 179.

2. I have been told that the culture portfolio would be a weak one in any cabinet. Surely this depends on the minister. One thinks of Charles de Gaulle's minister of

culture, André Malraux, a potent force in French culture at the time. Given the lobbying powers of the American cultural industries, we desperately need a strong cabinet figure to protect Canadian interests. To get a sense of how far such lobbyists will go, see Paul Gessell, "Heritage Minister Scores Political Points with Win over *Sports Illustrated,*" *Ottawa Citizen* Dec. 20, 1995. As for worries about the deadweight of "official" culture, the 1969 Commission des affaires culterelles in France made it clear that "The state helps culture, but there is no 'official' culture." See Bonnot 25-26.

3. See "A Fresh Look at Multiculturalism," editorial, *Globe and Mail* [Toronto] Nov. 29, 1994. "Mrs. Finestone argues that official multiculturalism now promotes tolerance and fights discrimination. Maybe so, but multicultural grants were $25.5 million in 1993-4." Naming the group grants I have listed, the editorial states that these are "Not big money, but borrowed money that we no longer have."

4. I am assuming that a strong federal ministry representing national cultural interests would make the commitment to decentralization I advocate in my "basic principles." On the need for a national information network, see Canada, *Art Is Never a Given* 27.

5. See Dizard ch. 9, app.

6. Marjorie Nichols, "Tory Guardians of CBC Tuned Out of Culture," *Ottawa Citizen* June 17, 1989.

7. "CBC-2 Tele-2A Proposal for National, Non-Commercial, Satellite, Delivered CBC Television Services," Aug.-Nov. 1980, *Report of the Federal Cultural Policy Review Committee* 290-91. The 1980 CBC proposal to the CRTC was opposed by a group called Lively Arts Market Builders (LAMB), G. Hamilton Southam chairman. It pointed out many deficiencies in the CBC proposals (for example, lack of provisions to support independent producers), and they were eventually shelved. (So were LAMB's.)

8. See "Feasibility Study for an Ontario Arts Campaign," report prepared for the steering committee of the Ontario Arts Awareness Campaign by Manifest Communications, Dec. 9, 1991. Here it is suggested that "arts awareness" campaigns be modelled after the well-known PARTICIPACTION campaign. It is suggested that merely advocating the arts is not enough; the audience, it is assumed, would seek the arts and contribute time and money if only it knew what the arts can offer. (Too much effort is used to convey what the arts *need.*) I believe the local-national network I am proposing here would be a useful vehicle – though not the sole required instrument – for putting the report's excellent ideas into effect.

9. Jay Stone, "An Explosive Mix of Arts and Politics," *Ottawa Citizen* Oct. 3, 1992. But see also Charlotte Gray 22 for some priceless anti-Council rhetoric.

10. Marianne Andrault and Phillipe Dressayre, "Government and the Arts in France," Cummings and Katz 30-31; see also the editors' summary (356); and Bonnot 27. Malraux's culture-house idea was not entirely successful. In the modified versions, the *centres d'action culturelle,* less emphasis was placed on showcasing the arts in grandiose local structures than on the human side of the arts infrastructure. Why not federal assistance in gathering independent artists' centres into a national network, and in funding wider access to existing facilities in order to produce the maximum performance flexibility for both well-established and marginal or "shoestring" arts groups? Such centres could also be launching platforms for promotions and incentives from the Ministry of Culture, and good vehicles for audience building. Faye Levine, who is suspicious of "culture barons," advocates a similar dispersal for the United States. See Levine, *The Culture Barons* (New York: Crowell, 1976) 301.

11. Although one might question some of its selection policies and perhaps its priorities, the Art Bank in many ways did a creditable job. Cf., for the Dutch government's handling of art purchases, Marlise Simons, "Dutch State Dumping Some Non-Masters' Artworks," *New York Times* Sept. 14, 1992.

12. See Paul J. Dimaggio, "Decentralization of Arts Funding from the Federal Government to the States," *Public Money and the Muse: Essays on Government Funding for the Arts,* ed. Stephen Benedict (New York: Norton, 1991) 220-21, 227-30. Dimaggio distinguishes between decentralization and horizontal division. We have a great deal of the latter in Canada, not necessarily to the benefit of our culture. We need more decentralization of funding and decision making – both of which I advocate here. Dimaggio points out that though the National Endowment for the Arts is perceived to fund both cultural institutions and "far-out" art, and the states perceived to support organizations and younger artists, these perceptions are somewhat stereotypical. A great many compromises and balancing acts take place – there as here. See also Wolfgang Ismayr, "Cultural Federalism and Public Support for the Arts in the Federal Republic of Germany," Cummings and Katz 45-47; Kleberg 180-83; and Andrault and Dressayre 41.

13. John Meisel and Jean van Loon, "Cultivating the Bushgarden: Cultural Policy in Canada," Cummings and Katz 295-99.

14. See, for example, Woodcock 88 on British Columbian "rednecks" who, at the time of the writing of Woodcock's book, had failed to support an arts council giving regular support to the (flourishing) arts in the province.

15. Godfrey, "Going Solo."

16. For a comprehensive overview of Canadian culture and foreign policy, see Cooper passim.

17. The kind of external cultural conflict we do not need is illustrated by the recently reported competition between two Paris bookstores, one Canadian-run and the other Quebec-funded. See Nico Columbant and Nick Spicer, "Le Battle of les Bookstores," *Globe and Mail* [Toronto] Dec. 16, 1995. This is precisely the kind of thing one might expect to see following Quebec separation, yet, as I stated earlier in this chapter, cooperation is really essential for both sides.

18. Saul 85-90.

19. Saul 95.

20. Saul 93.

Chapter 8: But Where's the Money to Come From?

1. Cummings and Katz 350.

2. Cummings and Katz 8.

3. Cummings, "Government and the Arts: An Overview," Benedict 46-49.

4. Jocelyn Harvey, "Variations and Innovations in Public Support of the Arts in Selected Countries" (Ottawa: Canada Council, 1993) 7.

5. Godfrey, "Artists."

6. Dwyer et al.

7. Dwyer et al.

8. Charlotte Gray. Yet Canadian artists, when pressed to it, are even better than their American counterparts in getting money from private sources. See Robert Everett-Green, "Top Marks in Fund Raising Provide Small Comfort," *Globe and Mail* [Toronto] Nov. 23, 1995. Everett-Green quotes Donna Scott as announcing a new mission for the Canada Council, namely, establishing connections between

artists and business, and interprets this (quite correctly, I think) as a smoke screen for planned government neglect.

9. Fulford, *Culture and the Marketplace* 43-56.

10. Coyne, qtd. in Fulford 44.

11. See Fulford 11-23.

12. Harvey 45.

13. Allan Gotlieb, speech to the Vancouver Board of Trade, Nov. 26, 1992.

14. Woodcock 194.

15. Harvey 41. The importance of finding new funding for the arts would certainly justify our first national lottery.

16. I owe these ideas to Jocelyn Harvey's excellent survey.

17. See "The Canada Council: A Design for the Future," Mar. 26, 1995.

18. Metcalf 44.

19. "So Who Reads Books? MP Asks," *Globe and Mail* [Toronto] Oct. 30, 1991.

20. Saul 115.

21. Dimaggio, Benedict 227-30.

22. See "Feasibility Study for an Ontario Arts Campaign."

Chapter 9: The Arts and Education

1. McIntosh et al. 20-22.

2. McIntosh et al. 103.

3. Working teachers in schools with large immigrant populations may find this chapter utopian. Nonetheless I believe they make a great mistake in assuming that they have to approach their students chiefly through the original ethnic culture. "Mozart doesn't reach them," we are told. Or, "We can't impose our own values." But Mozart does reach them, if well taught, and *should* reach them, just because his music is central to our culture which, we assumed and were happy to know, they had chosen as theirs. Why should we apologize for our traditions? Mozart belongs not to Austria or Europe but to the world. I have nothing against teachers reaching ethnic groups through what is familiar to those groups, but the purpose of education is, surely, to expand the mind, not to confirm the validity of what is familiar. Nor have we any obligation to assist lobby groups in promoting their own agendas; if we pay too much attention to them, we are in danger of creating a factionalized society. See also Frank Hodsoll, who argues that the arts should be taught (1) to give students a sense of our civilization; (2) to foster creativity; (3) to improve effectiveness in communication; and (4) to allow students to make discriminating choices themselves ("The Road Toward Civilization," *Why We Need the Arts* (New York: American Council for the Arts, 1988, 80-81).

4. Janet Farina, Churchill School, Ottawa. I heard about this teacher from the mother of one of her enthusiastic students. Ms. Farina is doing instinctively what the Decima researchers conclude is a necessity in promoting culture. "It is essential that excitement about the excellence of artistic work be better conveyed to what appears to be a willing and waiting audience" (*Canadian Arts Consumer Profile* xxiii).

5. Allen Frame, "Building Arts Programs, Brick by Brick," *New York Times* Aug. 7, 1994, sec. 4A: 22-23.

6. Janet Farina explained to me that she had no special training in art. See Isabel Vincent, "Arts Education Changes Urged," *Globe and Mail* [Toronto] Feb. 8, 1991, reporting on the Ontario Institute for Studies in Education Conference. Bronwyn

Drainie (I believe rightly) opposed the notion of special training for arts teachers. See also Cummings and Katz 358.

7. See Richard Courtney et al., *Teacher Education in the Arts* (Sharon, ON: Bison, 1985). See also McIntosh et al. 275-375, who summarize: "So the conclusion to the question 'Is arts education helping us to make informed choices in the arts?' is 'yes.' . . . To the question of whether those opportunities are equally available across the areas of the arts and in all regions of Canada, the answer is a qualified 'no'." The point is that many arts-education programs *are* available, but mainly in urban areas.

8. Postman, *Technopoly* 19-20, ch. 7. See also Andrew D. Miall, "How Do You Surf a Swamp?" *CAUT Bulletin* 42.10 (1995): 10.

9. For some of the implications of the ubiquitous new technology on the structure and values of Canadian society, see Heather Menzies, *Fast Forward and Out of Control* (Toronto: Macmillan, 1985); and Ursula Franklin, *The Real World of Technology* (Toronto: CBC, 1990). See also "More Study Needed," editorial, *Ottawa Citizen* Dec. 16, 1995.

10. Northrop Frye, in Canada CRTC, *Symposium on Television Violence* (Ottawa: Department of Supply and Services, 1976) 212; and Postman, *Technopoly* 197-98.

11. Postman, *Technopoly* 175-77.

12. Tim Lougheed, "Culture, Ideas and More," *University Affairs* 36.1 (1995): 52.

13. *The Common Curriculum: Grades 1-9* (Toronto: Queen's Printer, 1993) 18-21.

14. *Common Curriculum* 19.

15. *Common Curriculum* 21. See also Dennie Palmer Wolf and Mary Burger, "More than Minor Disturbances: The Place of the Arts in American Education," Benedict 118-52. They document the many ramifications of "art-learning," including affirming the notion that "to do art is to think." They point out how "doing art" acquaints the young person with the culture/art resources of the community.

16. The hostility of modern critics to biography is a measure of their fear of giving credit to the individual creator; "exclude the human and buoy up the theory at all costs" seems to be their motto, as if creative works were produced by abstractions.

17. Michael Polanyi and Harry Prosch, *Meaning* (Chicago: U of Chicago P, 1975) 109.

18. *Meaning* 99.

19. *Common Curriculum* 18.

20. Ludic, from the Latin *ludus,* "play." The importance of play in culture is best stated in the famous book by Johann Huizinga, *The Play Element in Culture* (Boston: Beacon, 1950). Liminal, from the Latin *limen,* "threshold." See V. Turner, *The Ritual Process* (Middlesex, Eng.: Penguin, 1974).

21. Consider the wonderful case of the bus driver from Tyneside, England, who was haunted by the face of Beethoven and eventually driven to become an enthusiast of classical music. See *BBC Music,* letters, Feb. 1993: 121.

Conclusion

1. Dubos 100.

2. Dubos 100.

Bibliography

American Council for the Arts. *Why We Need the Arts*. New York: American Council for the Arts, 1988.

Aspen Institute. *The Arts, Economics and Politics*. Aspen, CO: Papers of the Aspen Institute, 1975.

Audley, Paul. *Canada's Cultural Industries: Broadcasting, Publishing, Records and Film*. Toronto: Lorimer, 1983.

Bell, John. *Guardians of the North: The National Superhero in Canadian Comic Book Art*. Ottawa: National Archives of Canada, 1992.

Benedict, Stephen, ed. *Public Money and the Muse: Essays on Government Funding for the Arts*. New York: Norton, 1991.

Bissell, Claude. *The Massey Report and Canadian Culture*. The John Porter Memorial Lecture. Ottawa: Carleton U, 1982.

Bissoondath, Neil. *Selling Illusions: The Cult of Multiculturalism in Canada*. Toronto: Penguin, 1994.

Bloom, Allan. *The Closing of the American Mind*. Chicago: U of Chicago P, 1987.

Bloom, Harold. *The Western Canon: The Books and School of the Ages*. New York: Harcourt, 1994.

Burckhardt, Jacob. *The Age of Constantine the Great*. New York: Pantheon, 1949.

Canada. *Art Is Never a Given: Professional Training in the Arts in Canada*. Ottawa: Department of Supply and Services, 1991.

—. CRTC. *Symposium on Television Violence*. Ottawa: Department of Supply and Services, 1976.

—. Department of Communications. *Report of the Federal Cultural Policy Review Committee*. Ottawa: Department of Supply and Services, 1982.

—. *Minutes of Proceedings and Evidence of the Standing Committee on Communications and Culture*. Apr. 10, 1990. Issue 8. Ottawa: Department of Supply and Services, 1990.

—. *Minutes of Proceedings and Evidence of the Standing Committee on Communications and Culture*. Mar. 12; Apr. 11, 1991. Issue 21. Ottawa: Department of Supply and Services, 1991.

—. *Report of the Royal Commission on National Development in the Arts, Letters, and Sciences, 1949-51*. Ottawa: Department of Supply and Services, 1957.

—. *Report of the Special Joint Committee Reviewing Canadian Foreign Policy: The Position Papers*. Ottawa: Public Works and Government Services, 1994.

"The Canada Council: A Design for the Future." Mar. 1995.

"The Canada Council and Cultural Diversity." In-house paper of the Canada Council, 1993.

The Canadian Arts Consumer Profile: 1990-1991. Toronto: Decima Research; Les consultants culture, 1992.

The Canadian Encyclopedia. Edmonton: Hurtig, 1988.

The Common Curriculum: Grades 1-9. Toronto: Queen's Printer, 1993.

Cooper, Andrew Senton, ed. *Canadian Culture: International Dimensions.* Contemporary Affairs Ser. 50. Toronto: Centre on Foreign Policy and Federalism, 1985.

Courtney, Richard, et al. *Teacher Education in the Arts.* Sharon, ON: Bison, 1985.

Crean, S. M. *Who's Afraid of Canadian Culture?* Don Mills, ON: General, 1976.

Culture and the Marketplace. Ideas. CBC Radio, 1993. Toronto: CBC Radioworks, 1993.

Cummings, Milton C., Jr., and Richard S. Katz. *The Patron State: Government and the Arts in Europe, North America and Japan.* New York: Oxford UP, 1987.

Czitrom, Daniel J. *Media and the American Mind.* Charlotte, NC: U of North Carolina P, 1982.

Didsbury, Howard F., Jr., ed. *Communications and the Future.* Bethesda, MD: World Future Society, 1982.

Dizard, Wilson, Jr. *Old Media, New Media.* New York: Longman, 1994.

Dorson, Richard M. *Folklore and Folklife.* Chicago: U of Chicago P, 1972.

Dubos, René. *A God Within.* New York: Scribner's, 1972.

"Feasibility Study for an Ontario Arts Campaign." Report prepared for the steering committee of the Ontario Arts Awareness Campaign by Manifest Communications. Dec. 9, 1991.

Franklin, Ursula. *The Real World of Technology.* Toronto: CBC, 1990.

Gibson, Shirley Ann, ed. *The Cultural Imperative: Creating New Management of the Arts.* Proc. of a conference, the Association of Cultural Executives, Kitchener-Waterloo, Nov. 1-3, 1985. Toronto: Association of Cultural Executives, 1985.

Globerman, Steven. *Cultural Regulation in Canada.* Montreal: Institute for Research on Public Policy, 1983.

Harvey, Jocelyn. "Variations and Innovations in Public Support of the Arts in Selected Countries." Ottawa: Canada Council, 1993.

Helwig, David, ed. *Love and Money: The Politics of Culture.* Ottawa: Oberon, 1980.

Henry, William A., III. *In Defence of Elitism.* New York: Doubleday, 1994.

Hillman, James. *Revisioning Psychology.* New York: Harper, 1977.

Hirsch, E. D., Jr. *Cultural Literacy: What Every American Needs to Know.* Boston: Houghton, 1987.

Huizinga, Johann. *The Play Element in Culture.* Boston: Beacon, 1950.

Jewett, Robert, and John Shelton Lawrence. *The American Monomyth.* New York: Anchor, 1977.

Jung, C. G. *Aion: Researches into the Phenomenology of the Self.* Vol. 9, pt. 2 of *Collected Works.* Princeton: Princeton UP, 1959.

Kazdin, Andrew. *Glenn Gould at Work: Creative Lying.* Boston: Little, Brown, 1984.

Keats, John. *Selected Poems and Letters.* New York: Houghton Mifflin, 1959.

Kerckhove, Derrick de. *The Skin of Culture.* Toronto: Somerville, 1994.

Kroker, Arthur. *Technology and the Canadian Mind: Innis, McLuhan, Grant.* Montreal: New World Perspectives, 1985.

Levine, Faye. *The Culture Barons.* NewYork: Crowell, 1976.

Litt, Paul. *The Muses, the Masses and the Massey Commission.* Toronto: U of Toronto P, 1992.

Mander, Jerry. *Four Arguments for the Elimination of Television.* NewYork: Morrow, 1978.

McIntosh, R. D., et al. *The State of the Art: Arts Literacy in Canada.* Victoria: Beach Holme, 1993.

McLuhan, Marshall. *Understanding Media: The Extensions of Man.* NewYork: Signet, 1967.

Menzies, Heather. *Fast Forward and Out of Control.* Toronto: Macmillan, 1985.

Metcalf, John. *Freedom from Culture: Selected Essays, 1982-92.* Toronto: ECW, 1994.

Meyer, Marvin W. *The Ancient Mysteries: A Sourcebook.* NewYork: Harper, 1987.

Niebuhr, Reinhold. *The Irony of American History.* London: Nisbet, 1952.

Ostry, Bernard. *The Cultural Connection.* Toronto: McClelland and Stewart, 1978.

Page, Tim, ed. *The Glenn Gould Reader.* Toronto: Lester, 1984.

Pick, John. *The Arts in a State: A Study of Government Arts Policies from Ancient Greece to the Present.* Bristol: Classical, 1988.

—. *The Privileged Arts.* London: City Arts Series, n.d.

Postman, Neil. *Amusing Ourselves to Death: Public Discourse in the Age of Show Business.* NewYork: Penguin, 1985.

—. *Conscientious Objections: Stirring up Trouble About Language, Technology and Education.* NewYork: Knopf, 1988.

—. *Technopoly: The Surrender of Culture to Technology.* NewYork: Vintage, 1993.

Playfair, Guy Lyon. *The Evil Eye: The Unacceptable Face of Television.* London: Cape, 1990.

Polanyi, Michael, and Harry Prosch. *Meaning.* Chicago: U of Chicago P, 1975.

Powe, B. F. *A Climate Charged.* Toronto: Mosaic, 1984.

Rowse, Tim. *Arguing the Arts: The Funding of Arts in Australia.* Ringwood, Austral.: Penguin, 1985.

Sherman, Barrie, and Phil Judkins. *Glimpses of Heaven, Visions of Hell: Virtual Reality and Its Implications.* London: Hodder, 1992.

Skidmore, Darrel R. *Canadian-American Relations.* Toronto: Wiley, 1979.

Slotkin, Richard. *Gunfighter Nation: The Myth of the Frontier in Twentieth Century America.* NewYork: Atheneum, 1992.

—. *Regeneration Through Violence: The Mythology of the American Frontier, 1600-1860.* Middletown, CT: Wesleyan UP, 1973.

Turner, V. *The Ritual Process.* Middlesex, Eng.: Penguin, 1974.

Wolfe, Morris. *Jolts: The TV Wasteland and the Canadian Oasis.* Toronto: Lorimer, 1985.

Woodcock, George. *Strange Bedfellows: The State and the Arts in Canada.* Vancouver: Douglas and McIntyre, 1985.

Wurman, Richard Saul. *Information Anxiety.* NewYork: Doubleday, 1989.

Young, John E. *Global Network: Computers in a Sustainable Society.* Washington, DC: Worldwatch Papers, 1993.

Index

Making Your Views Known

Canadian culture has been well served by individuals and groups who address politicians on behalf of general or specific arts causes. Every Canadian has the right to become an advocate for the arts.

Any reader interested in pursuing this aspect of arts involvement, or seeking information about the arts in Canada, should be aware of the existence of the Canadian Conference of the Arts (613-238-3561), which publishes a useful directory of arts services organizations and keeps in touch with the needs of artists and groups in all parts of the country. Other organizations include: the Coalition for the Arts and Education (416-466-1345); the Writers' Union of Canada (416-868-6914); the Canadian League of Composers (416-964-1364); the Canadian Association of Professional Dance Organizations (416-964-3780); the Canadian Museums Associations (613-233-5653); and The Friends of Canadian Broadcasting (416-968-7496). You can also contact ad hoc groups, such as the recently formed Coalition to Save the CBC, which address specific crises. Any of these can be contacted for information about specific issues in a discipline. Your provincial arts council or community arts service groups will have useful addresses, telephone numbers, and updated information, and can fill you in on local issues.

Making a financial contribution, becoming a subscriber, or volunteering your time are probably the most direct and helpful gestures you can make on behalf of Canadian culture. If you like what your local artists are doing, patronize them. Writing advocacy letters to local councillors, to members of provincial legislatures, to federal MPs, or to local newspapers on behalf of the arts is a very useful activity. Joining a lobby group that is pursuing a specific goal is a deeper commitment, one that may be time-consuming, but which can also be very rewarding. Many books and pamphlets have been written on arts advocacy and lobbying; for further information, consult the reference desk at your public library; write, telephone, or fax your provincial arts council; or write the Canadian Conference of the Arts (189 Laurier Avenue East, Ottawa, Ontario KIN 6PI). For a convenient list of provincial arts councils and other government resources, call the the Writers' Union of Canada (see above) and ask for their information sheet, which will be of help to both writers and potential arts advocates.